Home Builder's Guide to Construction in Wildfire Zones

Technical Fact Sheet Series

FEMA P-737 / September 2008

FEMA

Federal Emergency Management Agency
U.S. Department of Homeland Security
500 C Street, Southwest
Washington, DC 20472

This document was prepared by

URS Group, Inc.
200 Orchard Ridge Drive, Suite 101
Gaithersburg, MD 20878

Acknowledgements

Federal Emergency Management Agency (FEMA)

L. Gina White, FEMA Region IV, Mitigation, Project Monitor

David Kennard, FEMA Region IX, Mitigation

Daniel Powell, FEMA Region IX, Mitigation

Dennis Tewksbury, FEMA Region I, Mitigation

Christopher Hudson, FEMA HQ, Mitigation

State of California

Ernylee Chamblee, California Department of Forestry and Fire Protection

Greg Griswold, California Department of Forestry and Fire Protection (San Diego Unit)

Tom O'Keefe, California Department of Forestry and Fire Protection (San Bernardino Unit)

Ken Worman, Governor's Office of Emergency Services

Local California Officials

Cliff Hunter, Rancho Santa Fe Fire Protection District

Clay Westling, City of San Diego

Bill Metcalf, North County Fire District

Technical Assistance Contractor Team

Christopher M. Barkley, PE, URS Group, Inc., Task Order Coordinator

Diana Burke, ELS, URS Group, Inc.

Sherry Crouch, PE, URS Group, Inc.

Michael Gayrard, URS Group, Inc.

Rich Schell, RPF #1978, RWS Consulting

Thomas L. Smith, AIA, TLSmith Consulting, Inc.

Chris White, Anchor Point Group

Cover photo: Anchor Point Group, Boulder, CO

Wildland/Urban Interface Construction

FEMA

Purpose

To provide information about wildfire behavior and recommendations for building design and construction methods in the wildland/urban interface. Implementation of the recommended design and construction methods can greatly increase the chances of a building's survival in a wildfire (see Figure 1).

Figure 1. A home in the wildland/ urban interface that survived a wildfire (Anchor Point Group, Boulder, CO).

Background

Wildfires are a common, natural, and essential occurrence in the forests, woodlands, brushlands, and grasslands of the United States. When conditions are acceptable, fire professionals use fire to revitalize the ecosystem and reduce accumulated vegetation that can fuel a wildfire under certain conditions.

Although the severity and timing of fire seasons vary widely from region to region, wildfires often pose a threat to lives, property, and resources. During an average fire season, hundreds of homes are damaged or destroyed by wildfire, and in extreme fire conditions, thousands of homes can be damaged or destroyed. Severe fire weather in areas with significant amounts of wildland fuels can lead to extreme fire behavior.

Wildland fuels vary throughout the United States. In the Pacific northwest and the Lake States, forests are the predominate wildland fuel. In southern California, chaparral brush predominates. The plains states have grass and oak woodlands, New Jersey has Pine Barrens, and the southeast has pine and hardwood forests.

Wildfires can damage buildings through direct flame contact, convection (heat that rises from a fire and creates a smoke column), conduction (heat that transfers through material such as metal roofs and railings), and radiation (heat from a fire next to the building). Wildfires can also create burning embers that rise in the smoke column and fall on buildings. Firebrands (large pieces of wind-driven, burning material) can be blown through windows or lodged against a building and lead to ignition of the building.

Traditional efforts to protect buildings from wildfires have focused on fighting the fire before it reaches the buildings. With the expansion of residential construction into previously undeveloped forests and wildlands, more buildings are now at risk from wildfires. Fighting or suppressing the fire is often difficult or impractical; buildings must therefore also be constructed to be fire-resistant. No building can be completely fireproof, but implementing the recommendations that are described in these Fact Sheets should greatly reduce the potential for damage to a building and greatly increase its chance of survival.

Construction in the Wildland/Urban Interface

The following factors affect the probability that a building will survive a wildfire:

- Topography and weather
- Defensible space
- Building envelope
- Community infrastructure

Topography and Weather

Wildfires generally follow or are driven by terrain and weather. Buildings at the top of a canyon or ridgeline, at mid-slope, or in a ravine have a higher risk for damage from a wildfire due to the interaction of these features with strong winds than at locations such as valley bottoms. When a construction site is selected, the topographic features on and surrounding a site should be evaluated for their potential contribution to the exposure of a building to a wildfire. A building's configuration and location on a site should be predicated on minimizing the risk from these topographic features.

See Fact Sheet #3, Selecting the Construction Site.

Defensible Space

Wildfires travel quickly in areas where vegetation is dry and abundant. A defensible space around a building can improve the probability that the building will survive a wildfire. A defensible space is an area where combustible material, including vegetation, has been treated, cleared or modified to slow the rate and intensity of an advancing wildfire and to create a safer area for fire-suppression operations to occur. Buildings surrounded by zones of non-vegetated areas or areas populated by fire-resistant vegetation are more likely to survive.

See Fact Sheet #4, Defensible Space.

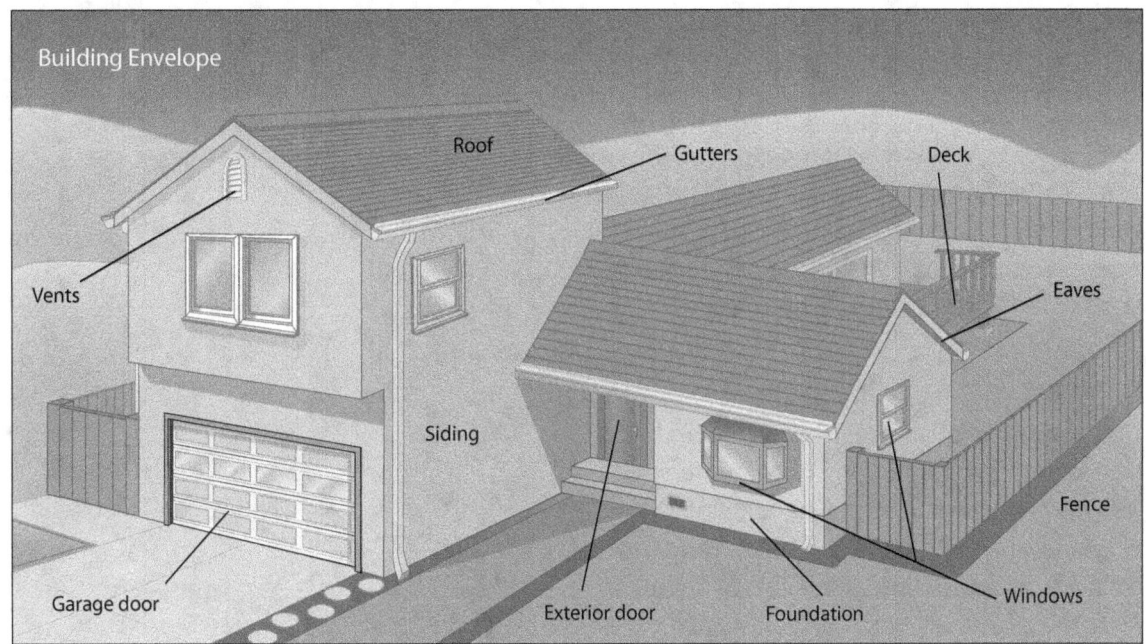

Figure 2. The building envelope.

Building Envelope

During a wildfire, combustible exterior building components such as roof coverings, siding, and decks can ignite, leading to severe damage to or total loss of the building. Therefore, the use of noncombustible or fire-resistant materials should be considered for exterior components. Figure 2 shows the components of the building envelope.

Also critical is the configuration of the noncombustible or fire-resistant materials. Unless construction measures that provide protection from a wildfire are implemented, heat and embers can penetrate the building envelope at vents, unsealed mechanical or electrical openings, and through windows broken by heat or wind-blown firebrands. When these openings are penetrated, the building can burn from the inside out.

If the envelope has been designed and constructed to be fire-resistant, both the exterior and interior of the building will be more capable of resisting a wildfire long enough for the danger to pass or for firefighters to arrive.

See Fact Sheets #5 through #16.

Community Infrastructure

A home that has been constructed to be fire-resistant and has a defensible space may not be sufficient to prevent damage from a wildfire. Surviving a wildfire may also depend on infrastructure such as local water resources for firefighting and roads that are designed for emergency vehicle access. The building site should also have adequate infrastructure to ensure access for firefighting crews.

See Fact Sheet #17, Community Infrastructure.

Prioritizing Fire-resistant Construction Techniques

The risk of wildfire varies greatly and depends on local fuels, weather, and topography. The risk at a building site must be determined before the appropriate design and construction methods for a new or existing building can be selected and the measures can be prioritized.

Hazard and Risk Assessments

The foundation of an accurate hazard and risk assessment is information on wildfire fuels, weather, topography, assets at risk, and the probability of a wildfire occurrence. A site can be in an area with a very high hazard (highly vulnerable to wildfire) but have a low risk of wildfire, such as a site at a high altitude. This information can be used to designate Fire Severity Zones. The zones can then be given a rating, from low to extreme, as shown in Figure 3.

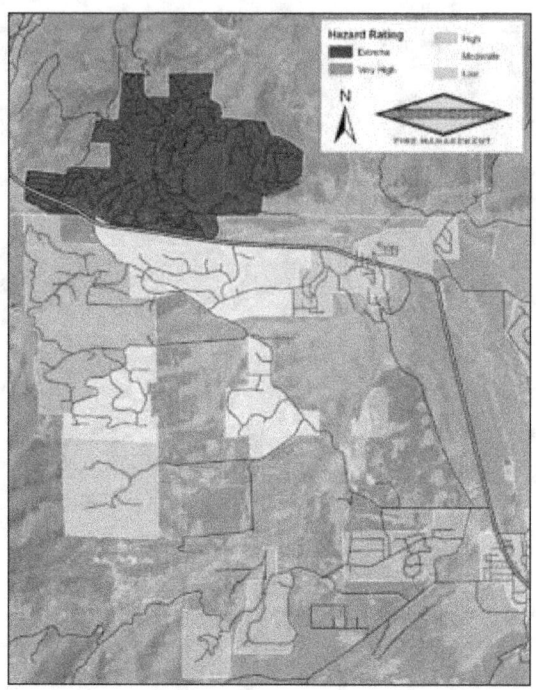

Figure 3. Example of a fire hazard rating map. Fire hazard ratings can help determine the level of mitigation that is necessary for wildfire management (Anchor Point Group, Boulder, CO).

A hazard and risk assessment can help determine the level of mitigation that is needed for a building. The assessment, which can be conducted at a regional, state, or local level, needs to be both credible and professional to ensure that the analysis is accurate, comprehensive, and verifiable. Some regional, state, and local agencies produce hazard risk maps similar to those shown in Figures 3 and 4. These maps may be found in state, tribal, and local agency hazard mitigation plans that have been approved by the Federal Emergency Management Agency (FEMA).

New Buildings

For new construction, FEMA recommends following the design and construction guidance provided in this series of Fact Sheets.

Existing Buildings

FEMA recognizes that it may not be financially possible for the homeowner to implement all of the measures that are recommended in this series of Fact Sheets. FEMA recommends that homeowners consult with local fire and building code officials or other fire management specialists to perform a vulnerability assessment and develop a customized, prioritized list of recommendations for remedial work on defensible space and the building envelope.

Helpful information about the vulnerabilities of the building envelope is available at http:// firecenter.berkeley.edu/default.htm. The Homeowner's Wildfire Assessment survey on this

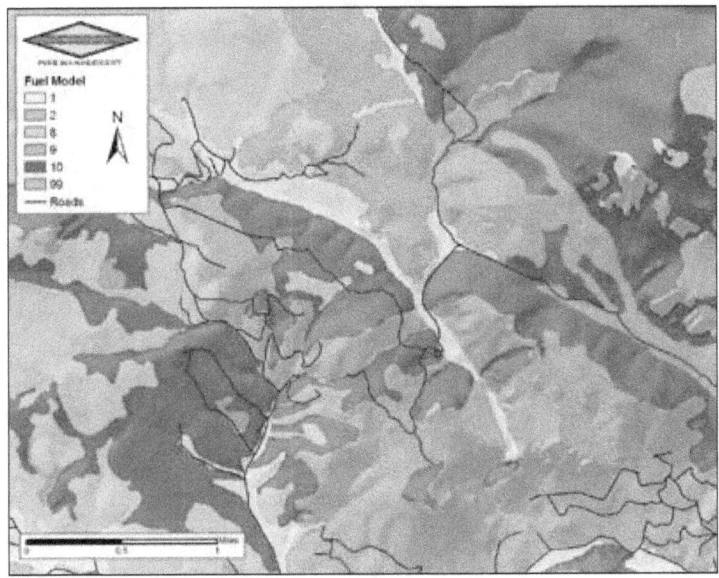

Figure 4. Example of a fuel model map. Fuel models that demonstrate the location of combustible vegetation are part of the foundation for fire behavior calculations (Anchor Point Group, Boulder, CO).

website is a helpful tool that property owners can use to learn about the specific risks a particular building has and the measures that can be taken to address them.

Construction Standards

Many communities enforce regulations regarding where and how buildings may be sited, designed, and constructed. The regulations, however, refer to minimum standards. Individual property owners have the option to exceed these standards, and doing so very often increases the probability that the home will survive a wildfire.

Resources

Center for Fire Research and Outreach. University of California, Berkeley: College of Natural Resources. http://firecenter.berkeley.edu/default.htm.

Christman, L. 2008. *Trial by Fire: Can Your Home Take the Heat?* Redding.com: Home & Garden. http://www.redding.com/ news/2008/Feb/16/trial-fire-can-your-home-take-heat/.

Underwood, J. 1995. "Fire-Resistant Details." *Fine Homebuilding* 96: 90–93. http://www. taunton.com/finehomebuilding/how-to/articles/fire-resistant-details.aspx.

Summary of Wildfire Construction Recommendations

State and local codes should include requirements for wildfire mitigation for both new construction and upgrades to existing buildings in wildfire zones. In areas where buildings are particularly vulnerable to the risk of wildfire, implementing measures that exceed the codes can improve the probability that a building will survive a wildfire.

The *Unified Hazard Mitigation Assistance Guidance* and the *Wildfire Mitigation Policy* for the Hazard Mitigation Grant Program (HMGP) and Pre-Disaster Mitigation (PDM) Program provide information on which activities are considered eligible for funding by the Federal Emergency Management Agency (FEMA) for wildfire mitigation activities.

This series of Technical Fact Sheets from FEMA provide information about how to minimize the potential for damage to or destruction of buildings in wildfire zones from wildfires. The information pertains to both new and existing buildings.

The Fact Sheets are available on the FEMA website (www.fema.gov) as Adobe Portable Document Format (PDF) files. You must have Adobe Reader to view the PDF files. The latest version of Adobe Reader is recommended and can be downloaded from www.adobe.com.

The following is a summary of the recommendations contained in Fact Sheets #3 through #17.

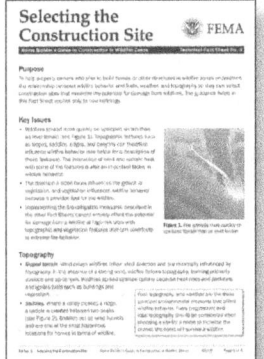

Fact Sheet #3: Selecting the Construction Site

Topographic features such as slopes and canyons, local vegetation, and weather can greatly influence wildfire behavior. Homebuilders should consider these factors carefully when selecting a construction site

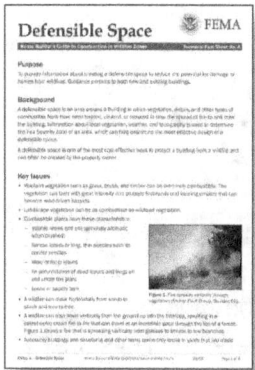

Fact Sheet #4: Defensible Space

Creating a defensible space, which can often be done by the homeowner, is recommended. A defensible space is an area around a home in which vegetation, debris, and other types of combustible fuels have been treated, cleared, or reduced. Landscape management creates a barrier between a home and a wildfire. Without a defensible space, firefighters may not attempt to protect the home because doing so would be too hazardous.

Fact Sheet #5: Roofs

Of the components of the building envelope, the roof is the most vulnerable in a wildfire because of its size and orientation. The probability that a home will survive a wildfire is greatly influenced by the components of the roof assembly. Class A rated roof assemblies with noncombustible coverings are recommended.

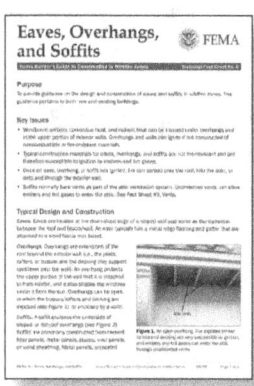

Fact Sheet #6: Eaves, Overhangs, and Soffits

Windborne embers and convective and radiant heat can be trapped near eaves and soffits, which can ignite if not constructed of noncombustible or fire-resistant materials. Eaves with short overhangs and flat soffits with a minimum of a 1-hour fire-resistance rating are recommended.

Fact Sheet #7: Exterior Walls

How well exterior walls are able to resist a wildfire depends largely on the materials used to construct the wall. Exterior wall coverings that are noncombustible or fire-resistant and not susceptible to melting are recommended. A minimum fire-resistance rating of 1 hour for the wall assembly is recommended

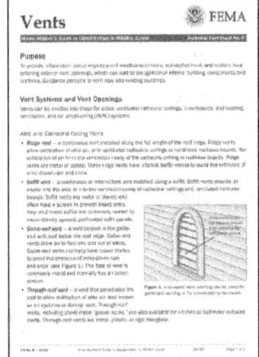

Fact Sheet #8: Vents

Embers and hot gases can be blown or pulled into vent openings and enter attic spaces, crawlspaces, and ductwork, leading to ignition of the interior of the building. Vents that are a minimum of 10 feet from property lines and other buildings, constructed of metal products, and have corrosive-resistant metal mesh screens are recommended.

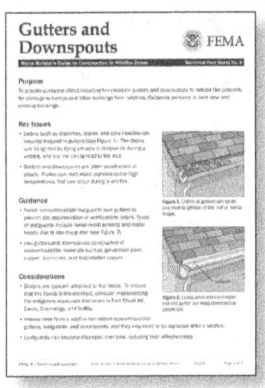

Fact Sheet #9: Gutters and Downspouts

Combustible debris such as leaves and pine needles can become trapped in gutters. The debris can be ignited by flying embers or firebrands during a wildfire, and the fire can spread to the roof. Noncombustible leaf guards over gutters and gutters constructed of noncombustible materials are recommended.

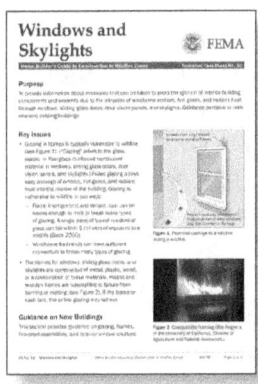

Fact Sheet #10: Windows and Skylights

Flames, firebrands, radiant heat, and failed frames can cause glazing to break or otherwise fail. Glazing (glass, plastic, or translucent material) that fails allows easy passage of embers and hot gases into the interior of a building. Insulated glazing units are recommended. The fire rating of window assemblies should be commensurate with the fire rating of the wall.

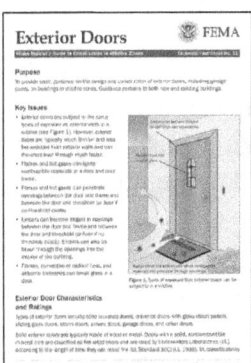

Fact Sheet #11: Exterior Doors

Combustible doors and frames can be ignited in a wildfire, and openings between the door and frame and glass in the door can be penetrated by flames, hot gases, or embers. The fire rating of the door should be commensurate with the fire rating of the wall. Weatherstripping and noncombustible or fire-resistant trim are recommended.

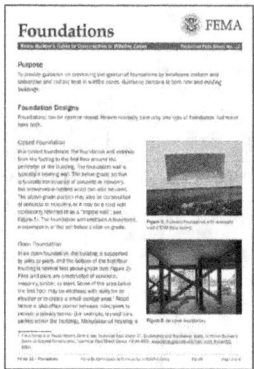

Fact Sheet #12: Foundations

Embers, firebrands, and hot gases can ignite combustible foundation walls and penetrate crawlspace vents and breached basement windows. Walls, vents, and windows in closed foundations should be constructed in accordance with the guidance in these Fact Sheets. In homes with open foundations, protecting the underside of the floor structure with fire-resistant materials is recommended.

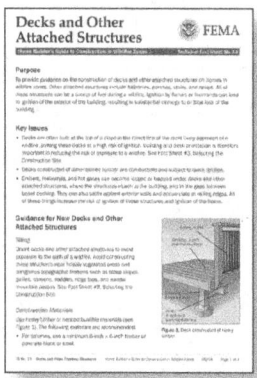

Fact Sheet #13: Decks and Other Attached Structures

Embers, firebrands, and hot gases can become trapped under decks and other attached structures. Decks constructed of heavy timber or noncombustible materials are recommended. Isolating the attached structure by surrounding it with noncombustible material such as gravel, brick, and concrete pavers, and enclosing the underside of the deck with fire-resistant skirting are also recommended.

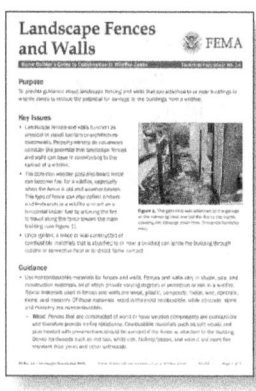

Fact Sheet #14: Landscape Fences and Walls

Once ignited, a fence constructed of combustible materials that is attached to or near a building can ignite the building. Fences and walls constructed of noncombustible materials such as concrete, stone, and masonry are recommended. Attaching a fence or wall to the building should be avoided unless the fence or wall is constructed of noncombustible materials

Fact Sheet #15: Fire Sprinklers

The interior of a building can ignite from a wildfire even when the exterior does not. Interior and exterior fire sprinklers can prevent substantial damage to the building, protect nearby buildings, and prevent the fire from igniting nearby combustible vegetation.

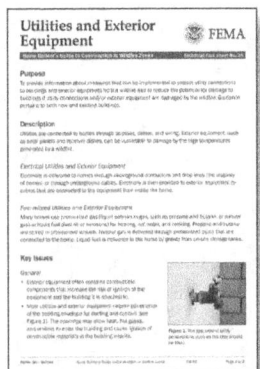

Fact Sheet #16: Utilities and Exterior Equipment

Most utilities require penetration of the building's envelope for ducting and conduit. Utility connections should be installed underground, if possible, and gaps and penetrations in exterior walls and roofs should be sealed with fire-resistant products. Fuel should be stored underground or surrounded by a noncombustible barrier.

Fact Sheet #17: Community Infrastructure

Access roads and driveways that are wide and strong enough to accommodate emergency vehicles and provide access for firefighting efforts are necessary. Water resources for wildfire suppression must be accessible. Roads and water sources should be well marked on signs constructed of fire-resistant materials for ease of use by emergency response personnel.

Selecting the Construction Site

 FEMA

Purpose

To help property owners who plan to build homes or other structures in wildfire zones understand the relationship between wildfire behavior and fuels, weather, and topography so they can select construction sites that minimize the potential for damage from wildfires. The guidance listed in this Fact Sheet applies only to new buildings.

Key Issues

- Wildfires spread more quickly on upsloped terrain than on level terrain (see Figure 1). Topographic features such as slopes, saddles, ridges, and canyons can therefore influence wildfire behavior (see below for a description of these features). The interaction of wind and radiant heat with some of the features is also an important factor in wildfire behavior.

- The direction a slope faces influences the growth of vegetation, and vegetation influences wildfire behavior because it provides fuel for the wildfire.

- Implementing the fire-mitigation measures described in the other Fact Sheets cannot entirely offset the potential for damage from a wildfire at high-risk sites with topographic and vegetation features that can contribute to extreme fire behavior.

Figure 1. Fire spreads more quickly on upsloped terrain than on level terrain.

Topography

- *Sloped terrain.* Wind-driven wildfires follow wind direction and are minimally influenced by topography. In the absence of a strong wind, wildfire follows topography, burning primarily upslope and up-canyon. Wildfires spread upslope quickly because heat rises and preheats and ignites fuels such as buildings and vegetation.

- *Saddles.* Where a valley crosses a ridge, a saddle is created between two peaks (see Figure 2). Saddles act as wind funnels and are one of the most hazardous locations for homes in terms of wildfire.

> Fuel, topography, and weather are the three principal environmental elements that affect wildfire behavior. Fuels (vegetation) and local topography should be considered when choosing a site for a home to increase the chance the home will survive a wildfire.

- *Ridgetops and hilltops.* Wind speeds on ridgetops and hilltops can be unpredictable but tend to be higher than those in the surrounding lower areas because of the higher elevation and because wind speed increases as it flows over abrupt changes in topography. Buildings in these locations can have 360-degree downhill exposure to wildfire.

- *Canyons.* A wildfire at the bottom of a vegetated canyon can lead to extremely hazardous conditions upslope. A canyon acts like a chimney, collecting hot gases and directing superheated convection and radiant heat upslope. Canyons funnel winds (see Figure 3) that can fan a fire and lead to extreme fire behavior (rapid spread of the wildfire and ignition of an entire area). An entire canyon can pre-heat from rising hot air and gases and explode in flames, creating a firestorm.

Figure 2. Wind behavior over a saddle.

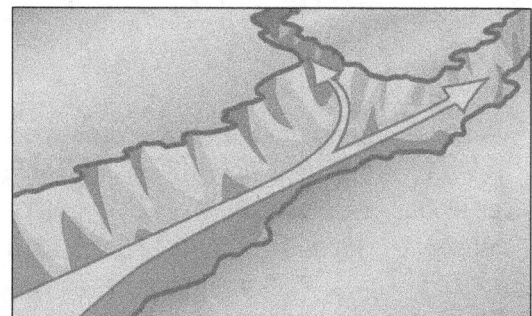

Figure 3. Wind behavior through a canyon.

Vegetation

- Vegetation acts as a fuel for wildfires. Vegetation both on and adjacent to a site can affect the probability of damage to a building from a wildfire. Characteristics of vegetation such as density, continuity, and type can influence wildfire behavior (see Fact Sheet #4, Defensible Space, for more information).

- South- and west-facing slopes generally retain less moisture, produce less vegetation, and dry out earlier in the year than north- and east-facing slopes. Fires on dryer slopes tend to ignite more easily, travel more rapidly, and burn out faster as light fuels are consumed. The more heavily vegetated moist slopes have a lower potential for ignition but can sustain a more intense fire of longer duration than dry slopes.

Guidance

By understanding how topography and vegetation can influence wildfire behavior, property owners can select construction sites in wildfire zones that reduce the potential for damage to a building from a wildfire. Following the guidance listed below can increase the probability that a building will survive a wildfire.

- Avoid selecting a construction site along a gully or in a narrow canyon.

- Avoid selecting a construction site in or adjacent to a saddle or narrow mountain pass.

- Avoid constructing a home adjacent to or on a steep slope. If a ridgetop site is selected, choose an area that allows for a minimum 50-foot setback from wildland vegetation on the downslope side (see Figure 4). Increase the setback at sites with heavier fuels such as in a forested environment. Implement the measures in Fact Sheet #4, Defensible Space; Fact Sheet #12, Foundations; and Fact Sheet #13, Decks.

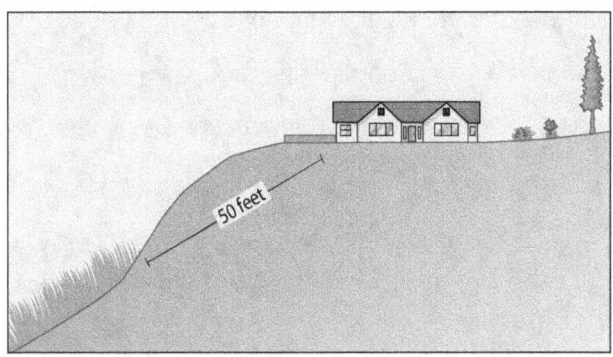

Figure 4. Example of setback from wildland vegetation.

- Orient the narrowest wall of the building toward the likely path of a wildfire to minimize the risk of structural ignition. Orient the building based on wind and fuels so that debris, embers, and firebrands do not accumulate next to the building's walls, especially near the inside corners of entries and other off-set walls.

- Minimize the number of windows on the side of the building facing the likely path of a wildfire to reduce the risk of radiant heat or firebrands and flying debris breaking the windows, allowing the fire to enter the building.

Considerations

- Consider the vegetation characteristics on and adjacent to the site including density, continuity, and type. If the site has heavy, continuous vegetation, a vegetation management plan may be needed to reduce the hazard. Creating a defensible space can enhance fire resistance (see Fact Sheet #4, Defensible Space).

- Consider access to the home. Steep driveways and narrow roads can limit accessibility by fire-fighting equipment (see Fact Sheet #17, Community Infrastructure).

- Evaluate the vulnerability to fire of neighboring properties. If the neighboring properties have fire hazards but the neighbors are unwilling to cooperate in developing a mutual defensible space, consider that information in selecting fire-resistance measures for the building.

Effectiveness

The effectiveness of the recommended measures can vary significantly, depending on the interaction of fuels, weather, topography, and wildfire behavior.

Resources

Barkley, Y.C., C. Schnepf, and J. Cohen. 2005. *Protecting and Landscaping Homes in the Wildland/Urban Interface.* Station Bulletin #67. Moscow, Idaho: Idaho Forest, Wildlife and Range Experiment Station. www.treesearch.fs.fed.us/pubs/22257.

California Department of Forestry and Fire Protection. www.fire.ca.gov.

California Fire Safe Council. www.firesafecouncil.org.

Firewise Communities Program. www.firewise.org/newsroom/faq.htm.

National Wildfire Coordinating Group. www.nwcg.gov.

Slack, P. 2000. *Firewise Construction Design and Materials.* Colorado State Forest Service.

Defensible Space

Purpose

To provide information about creating a defensible space to reduce the potential for damage to homes from wildfires. Guidance pertains to both new and existing buildings.

Background

A defensible space is an area around a building in which vegetation, debris, and other types of combustible fuels have been treated, cleared, or reduced to slow the spread of fire to and from the building. Information about local vegetation, weather, and topography is used to determine the Fire Severity Zone of an area, which can help determine the most effective design of a defensible space.

A defensible space is one of the most cost-effective ways to protect a building from a wildfire and can often be created by the property owner.

Key Issues

- Wildland vegetation such as grass, brush, and timber can be extremely combustible. The vegetation can burn with great intensity and produce firebrands and burning embers that can become wind-driven hazards.

- Landscape vegetation can be as combustible as wildland vegetation.

- Combustible plants have these characteristics:

  - Volatile resins and oils (generally aromatic when crushed)

  - Narrow leaves or long, thin needles such as conifer needles

  - Waxy or fuzzy leaves

  - An accumulation of dead leaves and twigs on and under the plant

  - Loose or papery bark

Figure 1. Fire spreads vertically through vegetation (Anchor Point Group, Boulder, CO).

- A wildfire can move horizontally from shrub to shrub and tree to tree.

- A wildfire can also travel vertically from the ground up into the treetops, resulting in a catastrophic crown fire (a fire that can travel at an incredible pace through the top of a forest). Figure 1 shows a fire that is spreading vertically from grasses to shrubs to low branches.

- Accessory buildings and structures and other items commonly found in yards that are made of combustible materials can also put an otherwise fire-resistant building at risk of ignition and destruction.

- Combustible vegetation and materials around a building (see Figure 2) can:

  - Increase the risk of building ignition

  - Restrict the space necessary to provide firefighters a relatively safe place to protect a building

  - Increase the chance that a building on fire will ignite adjacent wildlands

Figure 2. Combustible materials adjacent to a building create a hazard (Anchor Point Group, Boulder, CO).

Guidance

- Assess both the horizontal and vertical aspects of vegetation when designing the defensible space.

- To prevent the horizontal spread of wildfire, thin shrubs and trees so the crowns do not intersect and there is space between individual shrubs and trees.

- To prevent the vertical spread of wildfire, keep the lowest tree branches pruned and trimmed to maintain vertical separation from the top of shrubs and grasses to the lowest tree branches. The vertical distance needed will vary significantly, depending on the species of tree and composition of the understory.

- Create three concentric zones around the building (see Figure 3). Zone 1, the zone closest to the building, normally has the greatest need for fuel modification with progressively less modification in the other two zones. The higher the Fire Severity Zone, the larger the concentric zones should be. Consult the local or state fire agency for assistance. The three zones are discussed further below.

Zone 1

- Eliminate all combustible materials in Zone 1 (within 30 feet of the home) such as fire-prone vegetation, firewood stacks, combustible patio furniture, umbrellas, and dimensioned lumber decking (see Figure 4). Desirable substitutions include irrigated grass, rock gardens, stone patios, metal patio furniture, and noncombustible decking (see Fact Sheet #13, Decks and Other Attached Structures).

- Before fire season begins, remove combustible litter on roofs and gutters and trim tree branches that overhang the roof and chimney (see Fact Sheet #9, Gutters).

Zone 2

- Ensure that Zone 2 includes only individual and well-spaced clumps of trees and shrubs and/or a few islands of vegetation that are surrounded by areas with noncombustible materials.

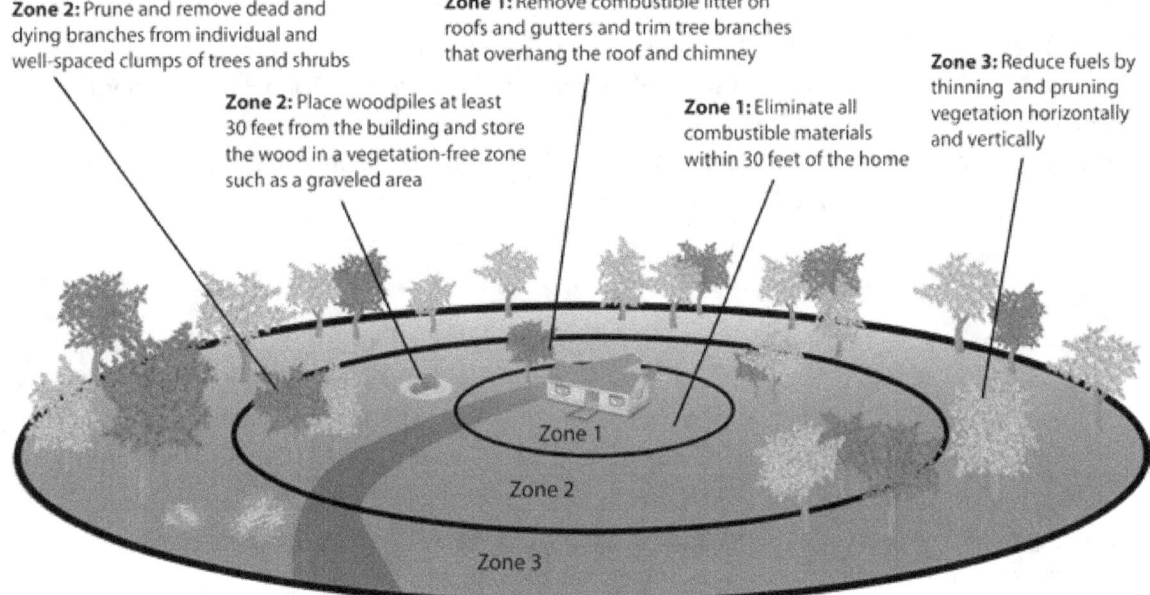

Zone 2: Prune and remove dead and dying branches from individual and well-spaced clumps of trees and shrubs

Zone 2: Place woodpiles at least 30 feet from the building and store the wood in a vegetation-free zone such as a graveled area

Zone 1: Remove combustible litter on roofs and gutters and trim tree branches that overhang the roof and chimney

Zone 1: Eliminate all combustible materials within 30 feet of the home

Zone 3: Reduce fuels by thinning and pruning vegetation horizontally and vertically

Zone 1

Zone 2

Zone 3

Figure 3. The three concentric zones of defensible space.

- Use hardscape features such as driveways and paved or gravel walkways or patios to create firebreaks throughout the yard.
- Plant fire-resistant, low-volume vegetation that retains moisture well and needs minimum maintenance such as pruning and removing dead and dying branches.
- Separate auxiliary structures such as a detached garage, pump house, pergola, and utility shed from the home by at least 50 feet. Increase the distance if the structure is used for the storage of combustible materials.
- Comply with recommended construction practices related to fire resistance for auxiliary structures. See Fact Sheets #5 to #16 for guidance on planning and designing a structure in a wildfire zone.
- Ensure that patio furniture is either made of noncombustible material such as metal or is at least 30 feet away from the building. Store patio furniture in a location that is protected from ignition by a wildfire.
- Place woodpiles at least 30 feet from the building and store the wood in a vegetation-free zone such as a graveled area.
- Store fuel tanks away from a structure at the minimum distance that is required by code or greater (see Fact Sheet #16, Utilities) and place underground or on a noncombustible pad.

Figure 4. A noncombustible ground cover in Zone 1 helped this home survive a wildfire (Anchor Point Group, Boulder, CO).

Zone 3

Reduce fuels that are farther than 100 feet from the building by thinning and pruning vegetation horizontally and vertically as discussed above. Thinning and pruning in Zone 3 can be more limited than in Zone 2. The goals in Zone 3 are to improve the health of the wildlands and help slow an approaching wildfire. Zone 3 is also an aesthetic transition between the more heavily modified Zone 2 and the unmodified surroundings.

Considerations

- Consult the local or state fire agency or qualified fire management specialist about codes, requirements, and standards related to defensible space. Codes, requirements, and standards normally represent the minimum that should be done. Consideration should be given to providing enhanced protection measures beyond the minimum recommended or required.
- Maintaining a defensible space requires routine maintenance of vegetation, which includes pruning and removing dead branches and leaves. Characteristics of low-maintenance plants are:
  - Drought-resistant
  - Pest-resistant
  - Native to the area
  - Noninvasive
  - Slow-growing
  - Wind-resistant
  - Sustainable without supplemental fertilization
- Vegetation modification must be performed in compliance with local, state, and federal environmental regulations.

Effectiveness

All mitigation measures listed in this Fact Sheet are effective in all Fire Severity Zones.

Resources

Barkley, Y.C., C. Schnepf, and J. Cohen. 2005. *Protecting and Landscaping Homes in the Wildland/Urban Interface.* Station Bulletin #67. Moscow, Idaho: Idaho Forest, Wildlife and Range Experiment Station. www.treesearch.fs.fed.us/pubs/22257.

Firewise Communities Program. www.firewise.org/newsroom/faq.htm.

National Fire Protection Association (NFPA) 1144: Standard for Reducing Structure Ignition Hazards from Wildland Fire. 2008. http://dnrc.mt.gov/forestry/Fire/Prevention/documents/WUIrewrite/ NFPA1144.pdf.

National Wildfire Coordinating Group. www.nwcg.gov.

Roofs

Purpose

To provide general guidance on the design and construction of roof assemblies on buildings in wildfire zones. Guidance pertains to both new and existing buildings.

Key Issues

- Roof assemblies are the most vulnerable component of the building envelope in a wildfire because of their horizontal orientation and size.

- Embers and firebrands can ignite the roof covering, other roof components, and debris on the roof. Once the roof has ignited, the fire commonly propagates into the interior of the building, resulting in substantial damage to or total loss of the building.

> **Roof covering:** The exterior roof cover or skin of the roof assembly (e.g., shingles, tiles, slate, metal panels, roof membrane).
>
> **Roof assembly:** An assembly of interacting roof components, including the roof deck, vapor retarder (if present), insulation (if present), insulation cover boards (if present), and the roof covering.

- The probability that a home will survive a wildfire is greatly influenced by the components of the roof assembly. The type and arrangement of the components govern their potential for ignition and their propensity to transfer heat into the interior of the building.

- The complexity of the roof's shape also influences the potential for ignition. A roof with valleys and roof/wall intersections where combustible debris such as leaves and needles can collect has more potential for ignition than a roof without them.

Fire-rated Roof Assemblies

The resistance of roof assemblies to external fire is rated by the American Society of Testing and Materials (ASTM), using test method E108. The method includes measurements of the surface spread of flame, the ability of the roof assembly to resist fire penetration from the exterior of the building to the underside of the roof deck, and the potential

> ASTM E 108 test conditions do not replicate actual wildfire conditions. In many cases, actual wildfire exposures are much more severe than those induced during the testing.

for the roof covering to develop flying brands of burning material. Roof assemblies are rated Class A (highest rating), B, or C. Assemblies that fail the test (do not meet the Class A, B, or C criteria) are unrated.

Class A provides the greatest degree of fire resistance, but there is a range of protection within the Class A rating. For example, some Class A rated assemblies have noncombustible roof coverings (such as clay or concrete tiles and metal panels), while others have combustible coverings (such as asphalt shingles and low-slope membranes).

Guidance for New Buildings

Many types of roof assemblies are rated Class A. Recommendations for various components of roof assemblies that are rated Class A are provided below.

> Only Class A rated roof assemblies are recommended for homes in wildfire zones.

Steep-slope Roof: Covering

A steep-slope roof is a roof with a slope greater than 3:12. The following design and installation practices are recommended:

- **Tile.** Clay and concrete tile are noncombustible and because of their relatively large thermal mass, retard the transfer of heat. Lightweight tile products are available, but normal-weight tiles are recommended because of their greater mass. If tiles are installed over wood battens, embers may be blown under the tiles and ignite the battens. Fire-retardant-treated battens are therefore recommended. If tile is used, the following are also recommended:

  - **Eaves, hips, and ridges.** Embers can be blown under tiles at the eaves, hips, and ridges. Birds can build nests in the space between the underlayment and the bottom of the tiles if the space is accessible, providing combustible debris that can be ignited by embers. Installing birdstops at eaves and fully mortaring hips and ridges are both recommended to avoid the accumulation of debris under tiles and to keep embers out (see Figure 1).

  Birdstops prevent debris from accumulating under tiles

  Figure 1. A birdstop at the eave.

  - **Valleys.** Unless special metal flashing is installed, combustible debris can accumulate in valleys and then under the tiles. Flat and plain tiles should be specified to be tightly butted to form a closed valley, and pieces of metal flashing should be installed under each tile course along the valley centerline. For profiled tile, lead or flexible flashing should be used, as recommended by the tile manufacturer (see Figure 2).

- **Metal shingles and panels.** Metal shingles and panels are noncombustible, but they readily transfer heat. If they are installed over wood battens, fire-retardant-treated battens should be specified and installed. If shingles or panels are installed over wood decking, 5/8-inch gypsum roof board complying with ASTM C 1177[1] should be installed over the decking.

- **Fiberglass-reinforced asphalt shingles.** Although a roof assembly that has fiberglass-reinforced asphalt shingles can be rated as Class A, these shingles contain combustible material (e.g., asphalt). If this type of shingle is used, a 5/8-inch gypsum roof board that complies with ASTM C 1177 over the wood decking should be installed for enhanced protection of the decking. Care needs to be taken when the shingles are nailed that the nails are not overdriven.

Figure 2. Special valley flashing to avoid debris accumulation between and below tiles (photograph courtesy of MonierLifetile).

- **Wood shingles and shakes.** Roof assemblies that have wood shingles and shakes can be rated Class A if the shingles or shakes are fire-retardant-treated and a specific cap sheet underlayment is installed. Without the underlayment, the maximum rating is Class B. Note that when shingles or shakes are fire-retardant-treated, they cannot be impregnated with preservative treatment.

If fire-retardant-treated shingles or shakes are installed over wood decking, installing a 5/8-inch gypsum roof board that complies with ASTM C 1177 over the decking is recommended in addition to the special underlayment that is required to achieve a Class A rating.

Steep-slope Roof: Underlayment

Embers can be blown under some types of steep-slope coverings such as tile, slate, and metal shingles and panels. If tiles become dislodged or cracked, embers can land on the underlayment below (see Figure 3). Installing an underlayment that has enhanced fire resistance is recommended to provide protection from embers that reach the underlayment.

Figure 3. Displaced tiles allow ember entry.

An example of an enhanced underlayment is a mineral-surface cap sheet that is rated for use in a Class A rated assembly.[2] If a mineral-surface cap sheet is used under metal panels or shingles, measures should be taken to prevent the metal from bearing directly on the cap sheet and the cap sheet from abrading the metal (thereby making the metal susceptible to corrosion).

---

[1] Boards that are 5/8-inch thick are type X ("special fire-resistant"). Boards that are 1/2-inch and 1/4-inch thick are not type X.

[2] Although cap sheets are normally the finished surface of a built-up or modified bituminous roof covering, a cap sheet can also be used as an underlayment.

Steep-slope Roof: Decking

Most homes have roof decks that are constructed of wood, typically plywood or oriented strand board. Fire-retardant-treated decking can be specified to avoid ignition of the deck. For more protection, 5/8-inch gypsum roof boards can be specified in addition to the fire-retardant-treated deck.

Although not common in homes, noncombustible decks such as steel or concrete, including concrete topping over steel decking, can be specified. In addition to being noncombustible, concrete decks offer great resistance to heat transfer and fire penetration through the deck from the exterior.

Low-slope Roof: Covering and Underlayment

Low-slope roofs have slopes less than 3:12. A variety of low-slope roof coverings and assemblies are available with a Class A rating.

If a low-slope assembly is selected, the following recommendations should be followed:

- Polyisocyanurate roof insulation should be specified (see Figure 4).

- A 5/8-inch gypsum roof board that complies with ASTM C 1177 immediately below the roof membrane (see Figure 4) should be specified.

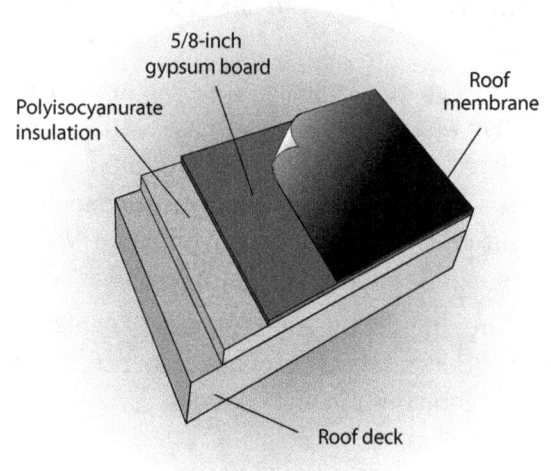

Figure 4. Components of a low-sloped roof.

- For enhanced fire resistance, in addition to the above recommendations, the roof membrane should be protected with heavyweight (i.e., 17 pounds per square foot minimum) concrete pavers (see Figure 5).

  - If pavers are placed over a built-up or modified bitumen membrane, a layer of extruded polystyrene insulation (intended for protected membrane systems) over the membrane should be specified.

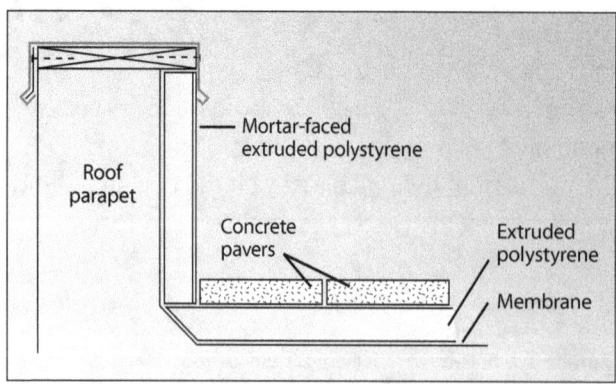

Figure 5. Concrete pavers over membrane (FEMA 55).

- Additionally, for smooth-surfaced built-up and modified bitumen membranes, a sheet of polyethylene (minimum of 4 mils) should be specified between the membrane and polystyrene to keep the polystyrene from bonding to the membrane.
- To protect the base flashings, a mortar-faced extruded polystyrene board should be installed over the base flashing (see Figure 5).

Low-slope Roof: Decking

Roof decking design and construction are the same for steep-slope and low-slope roofs. See the discussion under steep-slope roofs above.

Guidance for Existing Buildings

For homeowners with roof assemblies that are not Class A rated, the only long-term, reliable way to reduce roof vulnerability to wildfire is to reroof. Reroofing normally involves removing the materials above the roof deck and replacing them with new materials. The recommendations that are listed above for new buildings are applicable to reroofing design and installation.

Roof assemblies that have wood shingles or shakes and are not rated Class A and roofs with organic-reinforced asphalt shingles are vulnerable to a wildfire. These types of roofs should be replaced as soon as possible.

Considerations

- The homeowner should have roof debris removed from the roof surface and gutters regularly.
- Aging does not affect the ignition potential of tile. However, some roof coverings, such as wood or fiberglass-reinforced asphalt shingles, become more susceptible to ignition as they age. The roof covering should be replaced before deterioration of the covering significantly degrades resistance to ignition.
- Birdstops should be inspected annually to ensure that they have not fallen out of place.
- For recommendations on vents, see Fact Sheet #8, Vents.
- For recommendations on gutters and downspouts, see Fact Sheet #9, Gutters and Downspouts.

Effectiveness

All mitigation measures recommended in this Fact Sheet are effective in all Fire Severity Zones.

Resources

American Society of Testing Materials (ASTM). 2007. *Standard Test Methods for Fire Tests of Roof Coverings*. ASTM E108-07a.

FEMA. 2003. *Coastal Construction Manual*. FEMA 55.

Eaves, Overhangs, and Soffits

 FEMA

Purpose

To provide guidance on the design and construction of eaves, overhangs, and soffits in wildfire zones. The guidance pertains to both new and existing buildings.

Key Issues

- Windborne embers, convective heat, and radiant heat can be trapped under overhangs and in the upper portion of exterior walls. Overhangs and walls can ignite if not constructed of noncombustible or fire-resistant materials.

- Typical construction materials for eaves, overhangs, and soffits are not fire-resistant and are therefore susceptible to ignition by embers and hot gases.

- Once an eave, overhang, or soffit has ignited, fire can spread onto the roof, into the attic, or onto and through the exterior wall.

- Soffits normally have vents as part of the attic ventilation system. Unprotected vents can allow embers and hot gases to enter the attic (see Fact Sheet #8, Vents).

Typical Design and Construction

Eaves. Eaves are located at the down-slope edge of a sloped roof and serve as the transition between the roof and fascia/wall. An eave typically has a metal edge flashing and gutter that are attached to a wood fascia trim board.

Overhangs. Overhangs are extensions of the roof beyond the exterior wall (i.e., the joists, rafters, or trusses and the decking they support cantilever past the wall). An overhang protects the upper portion of the wall that it is attached to from rainfall, and it also shades the windows under it from the sun. Overhangs can be open, in which the trusses/rafters and decking are exposed (see Figure 1), or enclosed by a soffit.

Soffits. A soffit encloses the underside of sloped- or flat-roof overhangs. Soffits are commonly constructed from fiber-cement panels, metal panels, stucco, vinyl panels, or wood sheathing. Metal panels, untreated wood panels, and vinyl

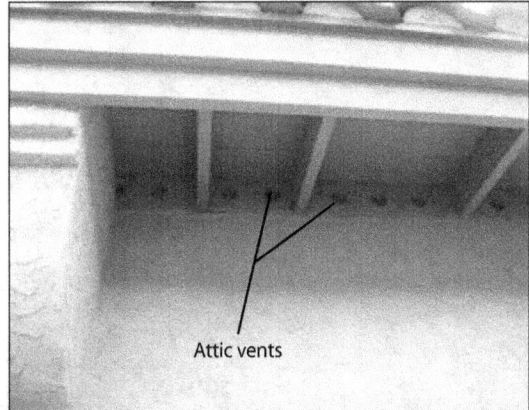

Attic vents

Figure 1. An open overhang. The exposed timber rafters and decking are susceptible to ignition, and embers and hot gases can enter the attic through unprotected vents.

panels are vulnerable to damage from wildfires. Metal panels conduct heat and can distort and allow passage of embers and hot gases. Untreated wood panels can ignite, and vinyl panels can melt and fall away.

Guidance for New Buildings

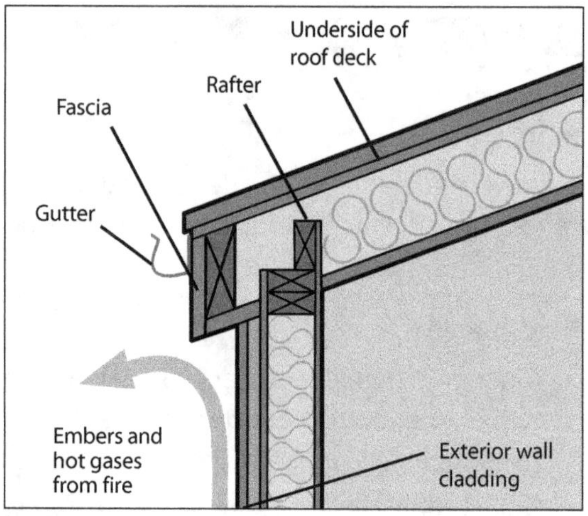

- Consider designing the building without overhangs (see Figure 2) to avoid the fire-related problems associated with soffits or minimize as much as possible the extent of the overhang to reduce the potential for entrapment of embers and hot gases.

- If no overhangs or short overhangs are unacceptable because of aesthetics or a desire to protect the walls from rainfall or windows from the sun, implement the following recommended measures:

    - Enclose overhangs with soffits that have a minimum 1-hour fire-resistance rating to prevent embers and hot gases from making contact with the joists, rafters or trusses, or the underside of the roof decking.

    - Use flat, horizontal soffits (see Figure 3) instead of attaching the soffits to the sloped joists, which creates sloped soffits. A flat soffit reduces the potential for entrapment of embers and hot gases.

- For the fascia, use noncombustible or fire-resistant materials (e.g., fire-retardant-treated lumber, fiber-cement board).

- For eave vents, follow the guidance in Fact Sheet #8, Vents.

Figure 2. An eave with essentially no overhang.

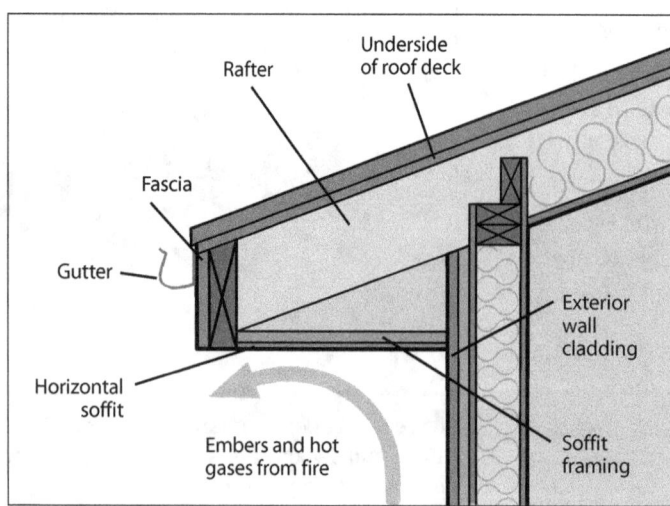

Figure 3. An enclosed overhang with a horizontal soffit.

Guidance for Existing Buildings

- Install a soffit under open overhangs according to the guidance provided above.
- Evaluate the fire-resistance of existing soffits and replace soffits that are not fire-resistant according to the guidance provided above. Some existing soffits (such as those constructed of plywood) can be covered with a noncombustible or fire-resistant material such as fiber-cement board or stucco.
- In very high Fire Severity Zones, install exterior 5/8-inch fire-resistant gypsum board between the existing and new soffit materials for enhanced fire resistance.
- If the fascia is combustible, cover the fascia board with a noncombustible or fire-resistant material (e.g., fire-retardant-treated lumber, fiber-cement board).
- For eave vents, follow the guidance in Fact Sheet #8, Vents.

Considerations

Planting combustible vegetation under eaves and overhangs should be avoided (see Fact Sheet #4, Defensible Space).

Effectiveness

All mitigation measures listed in this Fact Sheet are effective in all Fire Severity Zones.

Resources

Under Eave SFM Standard 12-7A-3, 2001 California Referenced Standard Codes (Part 12, Title 24, C.C.R.). http://www.fire.ca.gov/fire_prevention/downloads/Part_12_CA_SFM_12-7A-3_Test_Standards.pdf.

Exterior Walls

Purpose

To provide guidance on the design and construction of exterior walls in wildfire zones. Guidance pertains to both new and existing buildings.

Key Issues

- Exterior walls are susceptible to wildfire flames, conductive heat, and radiant heat. Flames and heat can ignite combustible wall coverings. When exterior walls ignite, the fire can spread to other components of the building such as the roof, soffit, windows, and doors, resulting in substantial damage to or total loss of the building.

- Windborne embers and firebrands are also sources of ignition. Embers can become trapped in cracks in walls, window openings, and door trim boards and ignite combustible materials. Windborne firebrands can ignite wall coverings.

Figure 1. Vinyl siding that melted and warped during a wildfire (firecenter.berkeley.edu).

- The fire resistance of exterior walls depends primarily on what the walls are constructed of and the amount of nearby combustible material. Some types of construction materials such as vinyl siding do not burn but can melt when exposed to high temperatures (see Figure 1), allowing the fire to reach the underlying wall components and penetrate the interior of the building.

Guidance for New Buildings

- For the best protection, ensure that exterior wall coverings are noncombustible or fire-resistant and not susceptible to melting. Concrete, fiber-cement panels or siding, exterior fire-retardant-treated wood siding or panels, stucco, masonry, and metal are recommended materials. With these coverings, the covering itself should not ignite and fuel the fire. Examples of the types of coverings that are not recommended are wood siding that is not fire-retardant-treated, vinyl siding, metal siding susceptible to warping, and an exterior insulation finish system.

- Ensure that the entire wall assembly has a fire-resistance rating tested in accordance with American Society for Testing and Materials (ASTM) E119. Although the above recommended types of coverings provide an initial barrier to flames, heat may pass through the covering and ignite underlying wall components. A fire-resistance rating indicates how long under test conditions a wall assembly can prevent flames and heat from passing through the wall. A minimum fire-resistance rating of 1 hour is recommended, but higher ratings provide greater protection.

- Comply with the requirements of the fire-rated assembly, including using the exact type of materials, configuration, and attachment used during the testing that established the rating.

- For exceptional fire resistance, use insulated concrete form (ICF) walls, cast-in-place concrete, or fully grouted concrete masonry units. If ICF is selected, use a stucco or masonry wall covering to protect the plastic foam forms.

- If fiber-cement or metal wall coverings are used, install one layer of 5/8-inch type X exterior gypsum board with taped joints underneath housewrap (see Figure 2). For fiber-cement siding, the gypsum board provides secondary protection if the siding decomposes and falls away during a fire. For metal panels, the gypsum board minimizes the transfer of heat radiated from the metal panels to other wall components.

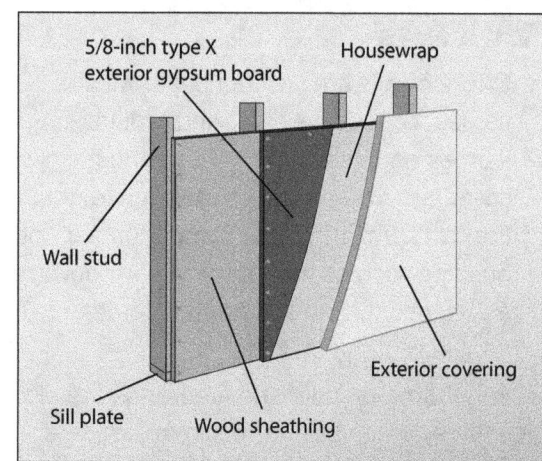

Figure 2. Example of a fire-rated wall assembly.

- For vinyl siding (note that vinyl siding is not recommended), install one layer of 5/8-inch type X exterior gypsum board with taped joints underneath housewrap. If the vinyl and housewrap melt during a fire, the underlying gypsum board will provide some protection.

- Use noncombustible or fire-resistant material such as exterior fire-retardant-treated wood or fiber-cement for trim boards around doors, windows, eaves, and corners.

Guidance for Existing Buildings

- Replace exterior wall coverings that are combustible, are susceptible to melting, or can readily transmit heat with one of the recommended coverings listed above. Examples of the types of coverings that need to be replaced are wood siding that is not fire-retardant-treated, vinyl siding, metal siding, and an exterior insulation finish system.

  - Before replacing vinyl or metal siding, check whether there is an underlying gypsum board substrate. If so, remedial work may not be needed.

  - Determine whether keeping the existing covering and covering it with 5/8-inch type X gypsum board and a new covering is a viable option.

Considerations

- For stud walls, metal studs can be used in lieu of wood studs. Metal studs do not ignite, but they transfer heat more readily than wood studs and can deform and collapse at temperatures that can occur in a wildfire. Current data are insufficient regarding the wildfire performance of walls that have wood studs versus metal studs.

- Maintaining and removing combustible debris (such as vegetation and leaves) and firewood near the exterior walls regularly reduce a building's vulnerability to ignition during a wildfire (see Fact Sheet #4, Defensible Space).

Effectiveness

A wall assembly with one of the recommended coverings and a minimum 1-hour fire-resistance rating is effective in all Fire Severity Zones.

Resources

ASTM E119 -08a Standard Test Methods for Fire Tests of Building Construction and Materials. http://www.astm.org/Standards/E119.htm.

Materials and Construction Methods for Exterior Wildfire Exposure: Exterior Wall Siding and Sheathing SFM Standard 12-7A-1, 2001 California Referenced Standard Codes (Part 12, Title 24, C.C.R.). http://www.fire.ca.gov/fire_prevention/downloads/%20Part_12_CA_SFM_12-7A-1_Test_Standards.pdf.

Vents

Purpose

To provide information about ways to avoid windborne embers, convective heat, and radiant heat entering exterior vent openings, which can lead to the ignition of interior building components and contents. Guidance pertains to both new and existing buildings.

Vent Systems and Vent Openings

Vents can be divided into those for attics; ventilated cathedral ceilings; crawlspaces; and heating, ventilation, and air conditioning (HVAC) systems.

Attic and Cathedral Ceiling Vents

- *Ridge vent* — a continuous vent installed along the full length of the roof ridge. Ridge vents allow exfiltration of attic air, or in ventilated cathedral ceilings or ventilated nailbase boards, the exfiltration of air from the ventilation cavity of the cathedral ceiling or nailbase boards. Ridge vents are metal or plastic. Some ridge vents have internal baffle media to avoid the entrance of wind-driven rain and snow.

- *Soffit vent* — a continuous or intermittent vent installed along a soffit. Soffit vents provide air intake into the attic or into the ventilation cavity of cathedral ceilings and ventilated nailbase boards. Soffit vents are metal or plastic and often have a screen to prevent insect entry. Vinyl and metal soffits are commonly vented by intermittently spaced, perforated soffit panels.

- *Gable-end vent* — a vent located in the gable-end wall, just below the roof ridge. Gable-end vents allow air to flow into and out of attics. Gable-end vents normally have louver blades to avoid the entrance of wind-driven rain and snow (see Figure 1). This type of vent is commonly metal and normally has an insect screen.

- *Through-roof vent* — a vent that penetrates the roof to allow exfiltration of attic air; also known as an eyebrow or dormer vent. Through-roof vents, including sheet metal "goose-necks," are also available for kitchen or bathroom exhaust ducts. Through-roof vents are metal, plastic, or rigid fiberglass.

Horizontal louvers can prevent embers from entering the ventilation system

Figure 1. A louvered vent opening can be used for gable-end venting or for connection to ductwork.

Crawlspace Vents

- **Crawlspace vent** — a vent installed intermittently through the foundation wall several inches above-grade. Crawlspace vents allow air to flow into and out of the crawlspace.

HVAC System Vents

- ***Through-roof vent*** (see above).
- ***Wall louvers*** — a vent opening on an exterior wall (see Figure 1). Wall louvers are connected to the HVAC ductwork where air enters or is exhausted from the building. Louvers are commonly metal. The louver blades are normally in a fixed position (i.e., cannot be rotated), but some have moveable blades that can be rotated to close the vent opening.

Key Issues

- Embers and hot gases can be blown or pulled into vent openings and enter attic spaces, crawlspaces, and ductwork, leading to ignition of the interior of the building (see Figure 2).
- Debris can accumulate at vent openings and ignite during a wildfire.

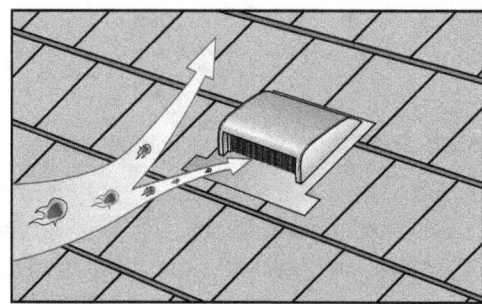

Figure 2. Embers or hot gases can be blown or pulled into vents.

Guidance for New Buildings

All Vents

- Specify and install noncombustible material for all vents. Metal products are recommended for vents and vent flashing.
- Specify and install corrosive-resistant, metal mesh screens with a maximum opening of 1/4 inch at all vent openings.
- Specify and install vent openings with a maximum net free area of 144 square inches.
- Place all vent openings at least 10 feet from other buildings or property lines to avoid ignition from embers and hot gases from an adjacent building that has ignited.

Attics (including Cathedral Ceiling and Ventilated Nailbase Boards)

Protecting attic spaces from wildfires is a challenge because air is naturally drawn into attics through vent openings. Although insect screens can prevent the entry of many embers, vent screens and louvers do not prevent the entry of hot gases. Vents that allow air to flow into and out under normal conditions and also avoid the entry of embers and hot gases in a wildfire can be provided in the following ways:

- ***Gable-end vent.*** Instead of using ridge vents, specify and install gable-end vents with specially designed metal shutters. When a wildfire threatens, the shutters can be placed over the gable-end vent. A hinged shutter that can be latched in an open or closed position is recommended (see Figure 3). A detachable shutter design can be used, but when the shutters are needed, the homeowner must remember quickly where they are stored. Shutters should have a gasket that provides a tight seal between the shutter and gable-end vent. For a more conservative shutter, a shutter with an insulated core encapsulated by metal (similar to a refrigerator door) can be used.

When gable-end vents are combined with soffit vents, effective attic ventilation can be achieved when the attic space is simple and relatively small, such as a small, gable-roofed house. If the house has a complex roof area or the attic is too large to be effectively ventilated by gable-end vents, ridge vents or through-roof vents should be used.

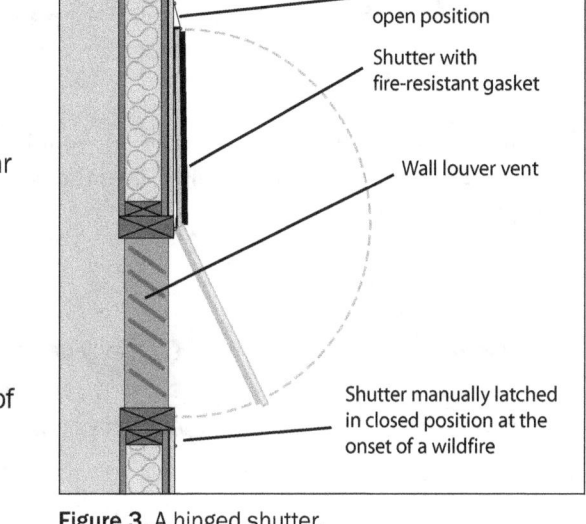

Figure 3. A hinged shutter.

- *Ridge vent.* Continuous ridge vents can provide effective ventilation, but typical ridge vents are not highly fire-resistant. Although air is normally exhausted through ridge vents, hot gases can enter the ridge vent and flow into the attic. Embers can also enter through the ridge vent if the vent does not have internal baffle media. Typical ridge vents are therefore not recommended unless the attic configuration or size requires ridge vents to ventilate the attic effectively. If ridge vents are used, metal vents with internal baffle media are recommended, but during a wildfire, the internal baffle material may melt and become ineffective at preventing embers from entering.

- *Soffit vent.* As with ridge vents, typical soffit vents are not highly fire-resistant, but because they are a necessary element of a vented attic, they cannot be eliminated. To avoid embers and hot gases from entering the vents, specially designed metal shutters over the soffit vent openings should be specified and installed. See the shutter recommendations for gable-end vents above.

- *Through-roof vent.* Through-roof vents are not recommended for attic ventilation because there is no known effective strategy for avoiding embers and hot gases from entering, other than blocking the vent. A 1/4-inch screen is effective at keeping out firebrands and embers that are larger than 1/4-inch but will not keep out smaller embers or hot air.

The Unventilated Attic
The most conservative approach to preventing embers and hot gases from entering the attic is to eliminate attic ventilation, but unventilated attics are controversial. Although allowed by the International Residential Code, provided the Code's criteria are met, unventilated attics may not comply with local building codes.

However, when unventilated attics are allowed by the building code or code compliance is not an issue, and when climatic and interior humidity conditions (e.g., no indoor swimming pools) are conducive to an unventilated design, an unventilated attic is a reliable way to prevent embers and hot gases from entering the attic.

Because of variable reliability of blocking techniques and the potential danger of homeowners falling from roofs while attempting to block vents, blocking is not recommended.

Crawlspace Vents

Specify and install specially designed metal shutters over crawlspace vent openings. A 1/4-inch mesh screen should also be installed over the vent opening. See the shutter recommendations for gable-end vents above.

HVAC System Vents

- *Wall louvers.* Specify and install specially designed metal shutters over wall louvers (see the shutter recommendations for gable-end vents above) or specify and install wall louvers that have adjustable tight-fitting blades that can be closed when a wildfire threatens.

  As an additional conservative measure with either shutters or adjustable blades, specify and install fire dampers within the ducts immediately behind the wall louvers. If sufficiently high heat penetrates beyond the louver, the fire damper will automatically close and prevent high heat from penetrating farther.

- *Through-roof vents.* As discussed in attic ventilation, through-roof vents are not recommended. Rather than running ductwork through the roof, extend the ductwork to an exterior wall where it can be fitted with a wall louver and shutter. If it is necessary to penetrate the roof, however, install a fire damper in the duct at the plane of the roof assembly.

Guidance for Existing Buildings

- If the home has ridge vents or wall louvers and they are not metal, replace them with metal vents according to the guidance provided above.

- If existing vent openings do not have screens or if the screen openings are larger than 1/4-inch, install metal screens according to the guidance provided above.

- Install shutters over gable-end vents, soffit vents, crawlspace vents, and wall louvers. If the existing wall or soffit is combustible, shutters may not be effective. In this case, installing shutters is probably cost-effective only if done in conjunction with upgrades to the wall or soffit.

Considerations

- Low-profile, through-roof vents have been used in place of soffit/eave vents with great success, but none of these products have been tested at the time of this publication.

- The homeowner should periodically have a professional remove debris that has accumulated near or on vent openings, vent screens, and louver blades.

- The amount of vegetation near vent openings should be limited (see Fact Sheet #4, Defensible Space).

- To minimize the possibility that embers and hot gas will be pulled into the home, the HVAC system, including exhaust fans, should be turned off when a wildfire threatens. Attic exhaust fans should also be shut down. Attic exhaust fans that are controlled by a thermostat may need to be deactivated by tripping the circuit breaker.

- For soffit construction, see Fact Sheet #6, Eaves, Overhangs, and Soffits.

Effectiveness

All mitigation measures listed in this Fact Sheet are effective in all Fire Severity Zones except as noted below.

- If a ridge vent is installed, the vent opening may be breached during extreme fire exposure by embers or hot gases, which could result in ignition of the attic.
- The effectiveness of shutter-protected vent openings is dependent on the deployment of the shutters by the homeowner prior to fire exposure.

Resources

Slack, P. 2000. *Firewise Construction Design and Materials*. Colorado State Forest Service.

Under Eave SFM Standard 12-7A-3, 2001 California Referenced Standard Codes (Part 12, Title 24, C.C.R.). Available at www.fire.ca.gov/fire_prevention/downloads /Part_12_CA_SFM_12-7A-3_Test_Standards.pdf.

Gutters and Downspouts

Purpose

To provide guidance about installing fire-resistant gutters and downspouts to reduce the potential for damage to homes and other buildings from wildfires. Guidance pertains to both new and existing buildings.

Key Issues

- Debris such as branches, leaves, and pine needles can become trapped in gutters (see Figure 1). The debris can be ignited by flying embers or firebrands during a wildfire, and the fire can spread to the roof.

- Gutters and downspouts are often constructed of plastic. Plastic can melt when exposed to the high temperatures that can occur during a wildfire.

Guidance

- Install noncombustible leaf guards over gutters to prevent the accumulation of combustible debris. Types of leaf guards include metal-mesh screens and metal hoods that fit into the gutter (see Figure 2).

- Use gutters and downspouts constructed of noncombustible materials such as galvanized steel, copper, and aluminum. Metal hood leaf guards are recommended because they do not melt and are relatively effective in keeping debris out of gutters (see Figure 2).

Figure 1. Debris in gutters can ignite and lead to ignition of the roof or fascia board.

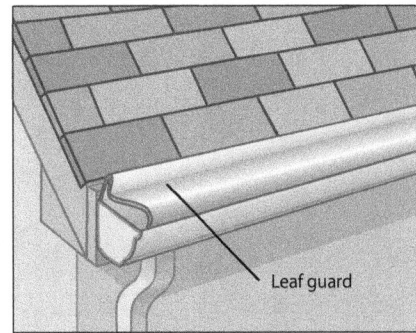

Figure 2. Leaf guards allow rainwater into the gutter but keep combustible debris out.

Considerations

- Intense heat from a wildfire can distort noncombustible gutters, leaf guards, and downspouts, and they may need to be replaced after a wildfire.

- Some leaf guards can become dislodged over time, reducing their effectiveness.

- Some types of leaf guards do not prevent all types of debris from accumulating in the gutter. For example, mesh-type leaf guards allow pine needles to accumulate. Leaf guards and gutters should therefore be checked regularly and debris removed if necessary.

Effectiveness

Noncombustible gutters, leaf guards, and downspouts are effective in all Fire Severity Zones.

Windows and Skylights

Purpose

To provide information about measures that can be taken to avoid the ignition of interior building components and contents due to the intrusion of windborne embers, hot gases, and radiant heat through windows, sliding glass doors, door vision panels, and skylights. Guidance pertains to both new and existing buildings.

Key Issues

- Glazing in homes is typically vulnerable to wildfire (see Figure 1). ("Glazing" refers to the glass, plastic, or fiberglass-reinforced translucent material in windows, sliding glass doors, door vision panels, and skylights.) Failed glazing allows easy passage of embers, hot gases, and radiant heat into the interior of the building. Glazing is vulnerable to wildfire in two ways:

  - Flame impingement and radiant heat can be severe enough to melt or break many types of glazing. A single pane of typical residential glass can fail within 5 minutes of exposure to a wildfire (Slack, 2000).

  - Windborne firebrands can have sufficient momentum to break many types of glazing.

- The frames for windows, sliding glass doors, and skylights are constructed of metal, plastic, wood, or a combination of these materials. Plastic and wooden frames are susceptible to failure from burning or melting (see Figure 2). If the frame or sash fails, the entire glazing may fall out.

Guidance on New Buildings

This section provides guidance on glazing, frames, fire-rated assemblies, and exterior window shutters.

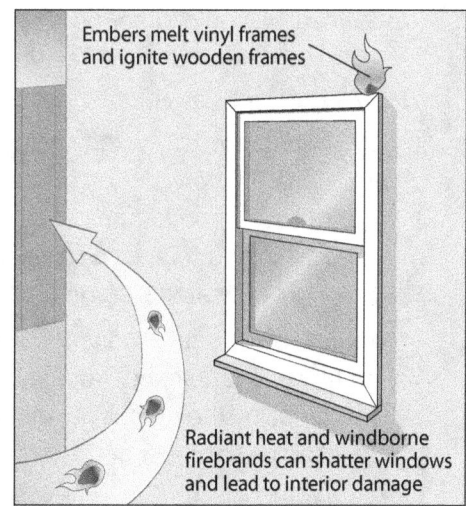

Figure 1. Potential damage to a window during a wildfire.

Figure 2. Combustible framing (firecenter. berkeley.edu).

Glazing

A variety of products are available for glazing in windows, sliding glass doors, door vision panels, and skylights. Glazing can be in a single- or multi-paned configuration. The recommended glazing products for homes in wildfire zones are laminated glass, tempered glass, glass with a low-emissivity, fiberglass-reinforced translucent glazing, and insulated glazing units (IGUs). Glazing products that are not recommended are annealed glass, ceramic glass, and plastic glazing.

Recommended

- **Laminated glass.** Laminated glass provides resistance to windborne firebrands. If a firebrand strikes with enough momentum to break the glass, the plastic film in the core of the glass will keep the glazing in the frame, allowing the broken glass to continue to resist firebrand impacts, embers, and hot gases. If the plastic film in the core gets sufficiently hot, the pane will delaminate whether or not the glass has been broken. If laminated glass is specified, it should either be protected by shutters, as discussed below, or combined with tempered glass in an IGU. See the information on IGUs below.

- **Tempered glass.** Tempered glass is more resistant to heat and flames than laminated glass or annealed glass (see below). The resistance of tempered glass can be enhanced with a low-e coating or a proprietary reflective coating, as discussed below. Firebrands with sufficient momentum can break tempered glass. To avoid breakage, the glass can be protected by shutters, as discussed below. Another alternative is to specify and install an IGU with a laminated glass inner pane.

- **Low-emissivity (low-e) coating.** Glass with a low-e coating provides a higher level of resistance to radiant heat than other types of glazing because the coating reflects radiant heat, reducing the probability that the heat will be able to enter the building. The coating should be on the inner surface of the exterior pane.

- **Proprietary fiberglass-reinforced translucent glazing.** This product is available for skylights and walls. The skylight material has a Class A rating. See Fact Sheet #5, Roofs, for a discussion of this type of rating.

- **Insulated glazing unit.** An IGU consists of two or three panes of glass that are separated by a sealed air space. Double-paned annealed units last about 10 minutes in a wildfire, twice as long as single-paned windows. In many cases, 10 minutes is long enough to provide protection from the fire. If the first pane fails, the second pane must still be penetrated (Slack, 2000) (see Figure 3). Laminated glass, tempered glass, and glass with a low-e coating can be combined in various ways into an IGU.

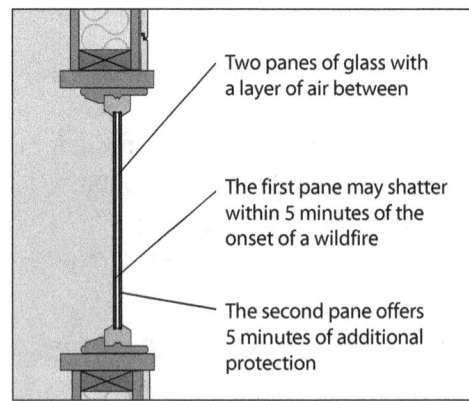

Two panes of glass with a layer of air between

The first pane may shatter within 5 minutes of the onset of a wildfire

The second pane offers 5 minutes of additional protection

Figure 3. Double-paned glazing.

Not Recommended

- *Annealed glass.* Annealed glass (also known as common float glass) is commonly used in residential windows. Annealed glass is the most susceptible to wildfires of the various glass types and is not recommended for homes in wildfire zones unless protected by shutters, as discussed below.

- *Ceramic glass.* This specialty glass is effective at resisting flames, but it transmits radiant heat readily. If ceramic glass is used for exterior glazing, heat that is high enough to cause ignition can be transmitted into the interior of the building. Ceramic glass is not recommended for homes in wildfire zones.

- *Plastic glazing.* Acrylic and polycarbonate are often used in skylights and sometimes in windows. Because plastic glazing can melt during a wildfire, it is not recommended for homes in wildfire zones.

Frames

A variety of products are available for window and skylight frames. To avoid window failure, frames should be constructed only of metal or metal-clad wood. Wooden and plastic frames should not be used.

Fire-rated Assemblies

If a fire-rated wall is specified, windows and sliding glass doors that are commensurate with the wall in terms of the fire rating are recommended. For example, a window with a 1½-hour rating is intended to be used in a wall with a 2-hour rating, and a door with a 3/4-hour rating is intended to be used in a wall with a 1-hour rating. However, a window with a higher fire rating may be used. See Fact Sheet #7, Exterior Walls, for information about fire-rated walls.

If a fire-rated wall is not specified, an IGU with a metal or metal-clad wooden frame should be used. See the information on IGUs above.

Exterior Window Shutters

Exterior window shutters can provide protection for windows and sliding glass doors in a wildfire. Solid metal shutters are unlikely to ignite or melt and are therefore recommended over wooden or plastic shutters (see Figure 4). For enhanced protection, an insulated metal shutter can be designed and fabricated. If the building is located in a windborne debris region within a hurricane-prone region, the shutter should meet the windborne debris criteria in the American Society of Civil Engineers standard, ASCE 7-05 (2006).

Figure 4. This metal shutter has top and bottom tracks that are permanently anchored to the wall (FEMA 577).

Guidance on Existing Buildings

- Windows and sliding glass doors, including frames, that are susceptible to damage from a wildfire should be replaced with the components that are recommended above and/or protected by shutters, as recommended above.
- Door vision panels that are susceptible to damage from a wildfire should be replaced with tempered glass with a low-e or proprietary reflective coating, provided the door has sufficient fire resistance (see Fact Sheet #11, Exterior Doors).
- Skylights with plastic glazing should be replaced with one of the recommended types of glazing, as described above.

Considerations

- Shutters protect the home not only from wildfires but also from extreme weather.
- Double-paned glass is more energy efficient than single-paned glass.
- A proprietary reflective coating is available for application to tempered glass. The coating acts like a low-e coating in that it reflects radiant heat, but the proprietary reflective coating may be more effective. For more information on this product and a comparison of fire ratings of various types of glass products and sizes, see www.safti.com.

Effectiveness

- Window assemblies with 3/4-hour minimum ratings are effective in all Fire Severity Zones.
- Metal cladding on metal clad-wood frames may become distorted during wildfire exposure and require replacement.
- Temporary shutters are effective only if the homeowner has sufficient time to put the shutters into place.

Resources

American Society of Civil Engineers. (2006). *Minimum Design Loads for Buildings and Other Structures*. ASCE 7-05.

Center for Fire Research and Outreach. University of California, Berkeley: College of Natural Resources. http://firecenter.berkeley.edu/default.htm.

Exterior Windows SFM Standard 12-7A-2, 2001 California Referenced Standard Codes (Part 12, Title 24, C.C.R.). http://www.fire.ca.gov/fire_prevention/downloads/ Part_12_CA_SFM_12-7A-2_Test_Standards.pdf.

FEMA. 2007. *Design Guide for Improving Hospital Safety in Earthquakes, Floods, and High Winds: Providing Protection to People and Buildings*. Risk Management Series, FEMA 577. http://www.fema.gov/library/viewRecord.do?id=2739.

Fire Rated Glazing Solution. www.safti.com.

Slack, P. 2000. *Firewise Construction Design and Materials*. Colorado State Forest Service.

Exterior Doors

Purpose

To provide basic guidance on the design and construction of exterior doors, including garage doors, on buildings in wildfire zones. Guidance pertains to both new and existing buildings.

Key Issues

- Exterior doors are subject to the same types of exposure as exterior walls in a wildfire (see Figure 1). However, exterior doors are typically much thinner and less fire-resistant than exterior walls and can therefore burn through much faster.

- Flames and hot gases can ignite combustible materials in a door and door frame.

- Flames and hot gases can penetrate openings between the door and frame and between the door and threshold (or floor if no threshold exists).

- Embers can become lodged in openings between the door and frame and between the door and threshold (or floor if no threshold exists). Embers can also be blown through the openings into the interior of the building.

- Flames, convective or radiant heat, and airborne firebrands can break glass in a door.

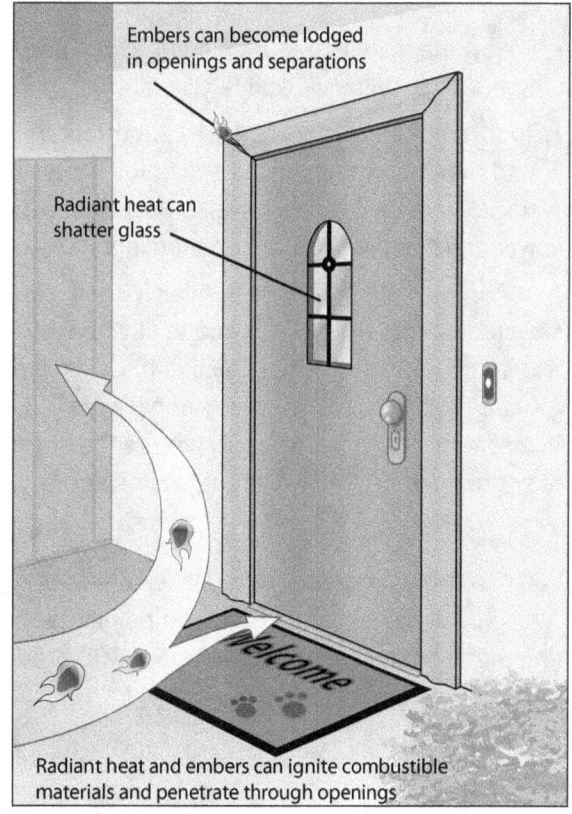

Figure 1. Types of exposure that exterior doors can be subject to in a wildfire.

Exterior Door Characteristics and Ratings

Types of exterior doors include solid entrance doors, entrance doors with glass vision panels, sliding glass doors, storm doors, screen doors, garage doors, and cellar doors.

Solid exterior doors are typically made of wood or metal. Doors with a solid, noncombustible mineral core are classified as fire-rated doors and are rated by Underwriters Laboratories (UL) according to the length of time they can resist fire (UL Standard 10C) (UL, 1998). UL classifications for interior and exterior fire-rated doors and their frames range from 3-hour to 20-minute ratings. Exterior fire-rated doors are available with a rating of 1½ hour or 3/4 hour.

The fire rating for doors is intended to equal three-fourths of the fire rating of the surrounding wall. For example, a door with a 1½-hour rating is intended to be used in a wall with 2-hour rating, and a door with a 3/4-hour rating is intended to be used in a wall with a 1-hour rating. However, a door with a higher fire rating may be used.

Guidance for New Buildings

- If a fire-rated exterior wall is specified (see Fact Sheet #7, Exterior Walls), specify and install a fire-rated door and frame. As explained above, the rating of the door and frame should be at least three-fourths of the rating of the wall. In addition, specify and install fire-rated hardware.

- Follow the guidance pertaining to door glass vision panels and glass sliding doors in Fact Sheet #10, Windows and Skylights.

- To avoid embers and hot gases penetrating the interior of the building between the door and the door frame, install adjustable weatherstripping on the interior side of the door frame and specify and install an automatic door bottom or threshold weatherstripping. The weatherstripping and door bottom should be tested in accordance with UL Standard 10C. Weatherstripping is relatively inexpensive (see Figure 2).

- Garage doors are typically made of wood, aluminum, or steel and are insulated or non-insulated. Unlike standard egress/ingress doors, garage doors are not normally tested for fire resistance (see Figure 3). To protect the garage door and entire building, follow the guidance listed below.

  - Specify and install insulated, metal garage doors.

  - To avoid embers and hot gases penetrating the garage, specify and install weatherstripping that has been tested in accordance with UL Standard 10C around the entire garage door.

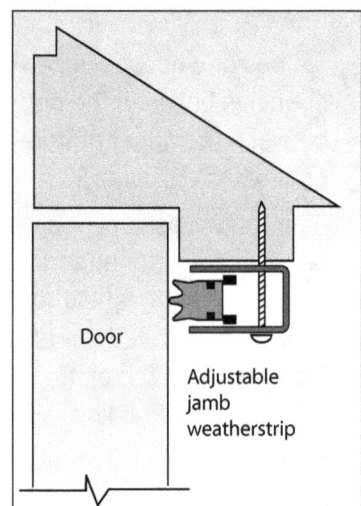

Figure 2. Example of adjustable weatherstripping (FEMA 577).

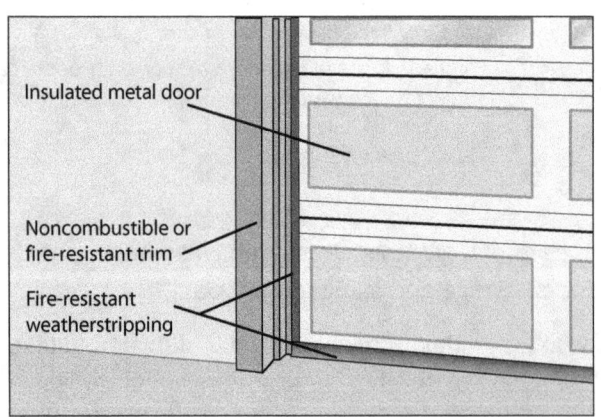

Figure 3. A garage door with noncombustible and fire-resistant components.

- For exterior trim that covers the opening between the door frame and exterior wall, specify and install noncombustible or fire-resistant material such as fire-retardant-treated wood or fiber-cement board.

Guidance for Existing Buildings

- Add weatherstripping to doors, as described above.
- Replace vision panels in doors, if necessary, as described in Fact Sheet #10, Windows and Skylights.
- Replace sliding glass doors and/or protect with shutters, as described in Fact Sheet #10, Windows and Skylights.
- Replace wooden garage doors, particularly if they do not have a solid core.
- Replace wooden egress/ingress doors without a solid core, although egress/ingress doors are often relatively fire-resistant compared to other components of the building and therefore not normally a high priority for remediation.

Considerations

Metal and metal-clad door frames can transmit heat during a fire, and the heat can ignite the surrounding exterior wall if the wall is not constructed to fire-resistant standards, as noted above. For more information, see Fact Sheet #7, Exterior Walls.

Effectiveness

All mitigation measures listed in this Fact Sheet are effective in all Fire Severity Zones except as follows:

- Garage doors are not normally tested for fire resistance and may not provide effective fire resistance in high Fire Severity Zones.
- Under very high heat or prolonged exposure to heat, weatherstripping material can melt or burn, lowering its effectiveness in preventing embers and hot gases from entering the interior of a building.

Resources

FEMA. 2007. *Design Guide for Improving Hospital Safety in Earthquakes, Floods, and High Winds: Providing Protection to People and Buildings*. Risk Management Series, FEMA 577. http://www.fema.gov/library/viewRecord.do?id=2739.

Steel Door Institute (SDI). 2001. *Basic Fire Door Requirements*. Technical Data Series SDI 118-01. http://www.steeldoor.org/res/118.pdf).

Underwriters Laboratory (UL). 1998. UL Standard 10C, Positive Pressure Fire Tests of Door Assemblies.

Foundations

Purpose

To provide guidance on avoiding the ignition of foundations by windborne embers and convective and radiant heat in wildfire zones. Guidance pertains to both new and existing buildings.

Foundation Designs

Foundations can be open or closed. Homes normally have only one type of foundation, but some have both.

Closed Foundation

In a closed foundation, the foundation wall extends from the footing to the first floor around the perimeter of the building. The foundation wall is typically a bearing wall. The below-grade portion is typically constructed of concrete or masonry, but preservative-treated wood can also be used. The above-grade portion may also be constructed of concrete or masonry, or it may be a stud wall (commonly referred to as a "cripple wall"; see Figure 1). The foundation wall encloses a basement, a crawlspace, or the soil below a slab-on-grade.

Figure 1. A closed foundation with a cripple wall (FEMA field team).

Open Foundation

In an open foundation, the building is supported by piles or piers, and the bottom of the first-floor framing is several feet above-grade (see Figure 2). Piles and piers are constructed of concrete, masonry, timber, or steel. Some of the area below the first floor may be enclosed with walls for an elevator or to create a small storage area.[1] Wood lattice is also often placed between piles/piers to provide a privacy screen (for example, around cars parked under the building). Manufactured housing

Figure 2. An open foundation.

---

[1] If the home is in Flood Hazard Zone V, see Technical Fact Sheet 27, Enclosures and Breakaway Walls, in *Home Builder's Guide to Coastal Construction*, Technical Fact Sheet Series (FEMA 499). www.fema.gov/rebuild/mat/ mat_fema499.shtm.

is typically supported on an open foundation, but often a non-bearing wall (skirting) is installed around the perimeter of the home between grade and the floor.

Key Issues

Closed Foundation

- Direct flame, embers, or hot gases can enter through crawlspace vents or breached basement windows.
- The crawlspace wall or wall covering or the exposed portion of the basement wall or wall covering can be ignited by direct flame, embers, or hot gases. Once the wall is ignited, the fire can penetrate the crawlspace or basement and climb up the exterior wall.
- Combustible items stored in basements or crawlspaces (such as household goods in cardboard boxes) can become fuel in a fire.

Open Foundation

- The underside of the first floor can be ignited by direct flame, embers, or hot gases. When piles or piers are constructed of timber, the pile/pier is normally thick enough to resist ignition. See Fact Sheet #13, Decks and Other Attached Structures, for information on ignition resistance as a function of timber width.
- Wood lattice screens can be ignited by direct flame, embers, or hot gases. Lattice screens often trap combustible debris such as leaves and paper, increasing the potential for ignition. Ignition of a lattice screen can lead to ignition of the underside of the first floor.
- Walls and wall coverings around enclosures such as elevator shafts and storage areas can be ignited by embers or hot gases, leading to ignition of the underside of the first floor.
- Combustible debris or storage items (such as firewood or gas in a container) in an open foundation can be ignited, leading to ignition of the underside of the first floor.
- Skirting around the perimeter of manufactured homes can be ignited, leading to ignition of the underside of the floor and spread of a fire up the exterior wall.

Guidance for New Buildings

Closed Foundation

- See Fact Sheet #7, Exterior Walls, for guidance on walls and wall coverings.
- See Fact Sheet #8, Vents, for guidance on crawlspace vents.
- See Fact Sheet #10, Windows and Skylights, for guidance on windows.

Open Foundation

To avoid ignition of the first-floor framing members (joists) and floor decking, sheath the underside of the framing as follows:

- Attach 5/8-inch thick exterior type X gypsum board to the underside of the joists. For energy conservation, install batt insulation between the joists (see Figure 3).

- Attach fire-retardant-treated plywood, fiber-cement panels, or metal siding panels over the gypsum board.

- Do not install lattice screens. If screens are installed, use chain-link fencing with metal privacy slats instead of wood.

- For guidance on enclosure walls around storage areas and for skirting on manufactured homes, see Fact Sheet #7, Exterior Walls. For guidance

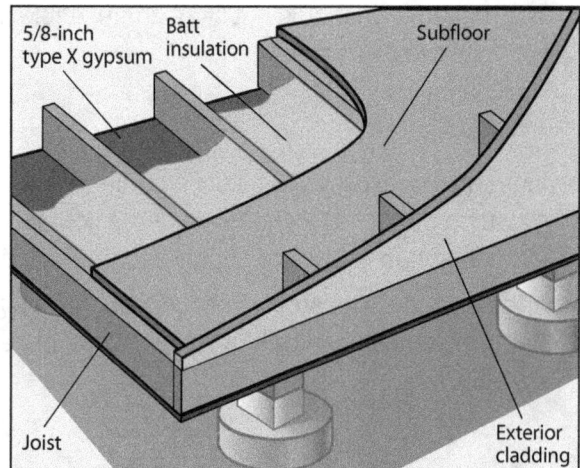

Figure 3. A 5/8-inch type X gypsum board attached to the underside of the joists.

on windows, see Fact Sheet #10, Windows and Skylights. For guidance on doors, see Fact Sheet #11, Exterior Doors.

Guidance for Existing Buildings

Closed Foundation

- See Fact Sheet #7, Exterior Walls, for guidance on walls and wall coverings.
- See Fact Sheet #8, Vents, for guidance on crawlspace vents.
- See Fact Sheet #10, Windows and Skylights, for guidance on windows.

Open Foundation

- If the first-floor framing members are timber members less than 3 inches thick (nominal) or if the floor decking is combustible, sheath the underside of the framing as described above.
- Evaluate floor beams and joists that are constructed of steel (not common in residential construction). Depending on a variety of conditions, it may be prudent to sheath the underside of the framing as described above or protect the steel with suitable fireproofing.
- Remove existing lattice screens or replace them with chain-link fencing with metal privacy slats.
- For guidance on enclosure walls around storage areas and for skirting on manufactured homes, see Fact Sheet #7, Exterior Walls. For guidance on windows, see Fact Sheet #10, Windows and Skylights. For guidance on doors, see Fact Sheet #11, Exterior Doors.

Considerations

- The homeowner should periodically remove combustible debris under buildings with open foundations.

- The homeowner should not store combustible items such as gas and firewood under buildings with open foundations.
- If a building is exposed to a wildfire, an engineer should evaluate the structural integrity of the foundation.
- In areas where dry rot is a concern, fire-retardant-treated plywood can be attached over the gypsum board on the underside of the floor joists, but plywood is affected more by weather elements than fiber-cement panels or metal siding panels.
- If the building is located in a floodplain, as designated by FEMA's National Flood Insurance Program, criteria set forth in Title 44 Code of Federal Regulations Part 60 should be considered.

Effectiveness

All measures listed in this Fact Sheet are effective in all Fire Severity Zones.

Resources

FEMA. 2005. *Home Builder's Guide to Coastal Construction Technical Fact Sheet Series.* FEMA 499. http://www.fema.gov/rebuild/mat/mat_fema499.shtm.

FEMA. 2006. *Recommended Residential Construction for the Gulf Coast: Building on Strong and Safe Foundations.* FEMA 550. www.fema.gov/library/viewRecord.do?id=1853.

Slack, P. 2000. *Firewise Construction Design and Materials.* Colorado State Forest Service.

Decks and Other Attached Structures

 **FEMA**

Purpose

To provide guidance on the construction of decks and other attached structures on homes in wildfire zones. Other attached structures include balconies, porches, stairs, and ramps. All of these structures can be a source of fuel during a wildfire. Ignition by flames or firebrands can lead to ignition of the exterior of the building, resulting in substantial damage to or total loss of the building.

Key Issues

- Decks are often built at the top of a slope in the direct line of the most likely approach of a wildfire, putting these decks at a high risk of ignition. Building and deck orientation is therefore important in reducing the risk of exposure to a wildfire (see Fact Sheet #3, Selecting the Construction Site).

- Decks constructed of dimensioned lumber are combustible and subject to quick ignition.

- Embers, firebrands, and hot gases can become lodged or trapped under decks and other attached structures, where the structures attach to the building, and in the gaps between board decking. They can also settle against exterior walls and accumulate at railing edges. All of these things increase the risk of ignition of these structures and ignition of the home.

Guidance for New Decks and Other Attached Structures

Siting

Orient decks and other attached structures to avoid exposure to the path of a wildfire. Avoid constructing these structures near heavily vegetated areas and topographic features such as steep slopes, gullies, canyons, saddles, ridge tops, and narrow mountain passes (see Fact Sheet #3, Selecting the Construction Site).

Construction Materials

Use heavy timber or noncombustible materials (see Figure 1). The following materials are recommended:

- For columns, use a minimum 6-inch × 6-inch timber *or* concrete block or steel.

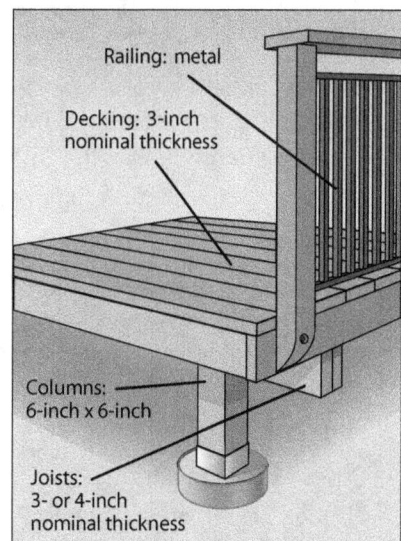

Figure 1. Deck constructed of heavy timber.

- For floor joists and beams, use heavy timber, 3-inch to 4-inch nominal thickness fire-retardant-treated wood, *or* concrete block or steel framing.
- For railings, use minimum 3-inch nominal thickness fire-retardant-treated wood *or* metal, cables, or tempered glass.
- For decking and stair treads, use exterior fire-retardant-treated wood, minimum 3-inch nominal thickness, *or* brick or concrete pavers and a suitable drainage mat over wood decking *or* metal grates. Light, poured concrete may also be a suitable deck covering.

Due to insufficient data comparing the performance of plastic and composite materials to heavy timber decking when exposed to flames and heat, FEMA does not recommend the use of plastic or composite decking in high Fire Severity Zones. However, the University of California's Center for Fire Research and Outreach (Berkeley) has conducted some testing on plastic and composite materials used in decks. Results are as follows:

- Plastic and composite products with channels on the underside of the decking degraded early when exposed to under-deck fires.
- Products with hollow construction exhibited board collapse when exposed to firebrands.
- Some products with a solid construction performed similarly to 2-inch thick nominal wood decking, but many did not perform as well as heavy timber decking.

More information on the testing is available at http://www.fire.ca.gov/fire_prevention/downloads/Part_12_CA_SFM_12-7A-4_Test_Standards.pdf.

Construction Techniques

- Isolate the attached structure by surrounding it with noncombustible material such as gravel, brick, or concrete pavers to prevent vegetative growth and reduce fuel in a wildfire (see Figure 2).
- Enclose the underside of the deck with fire-resistant skirting that acts as a shield against embers and reduces the probability that radiated and convected heat will ignite the deck (see Figure 2).
- To prevent ember intrusion in gaps between the decking and home (such as in offset ledger board construction), cover the gaps with 1/8-inch metal screening. Install flashing on ledger boards that are attached without gaps to create a barrier to embers and prevent water from penetrating (see Figure 3).
- Cover exposed floor framing at the underside of attached structures with a fire-resistant soffit such as fiber-cement panels. The soffit should have weep holes with a maximum diameter of 1/4 inch to allow water that leaks through the decking to drain out of the soffit space.

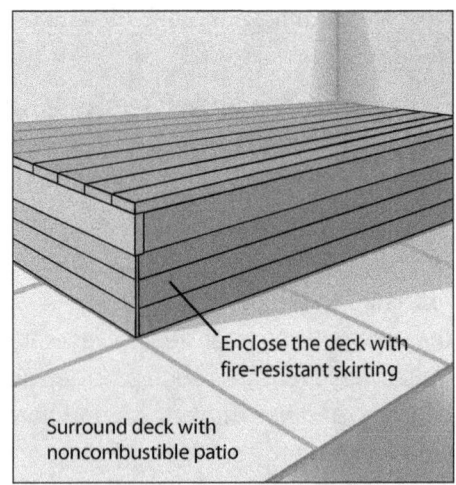

Enclose the deck with fire-resistant skirting

Surround deck with noncombustible patio

Figure 2. Deck isolated by a patio.

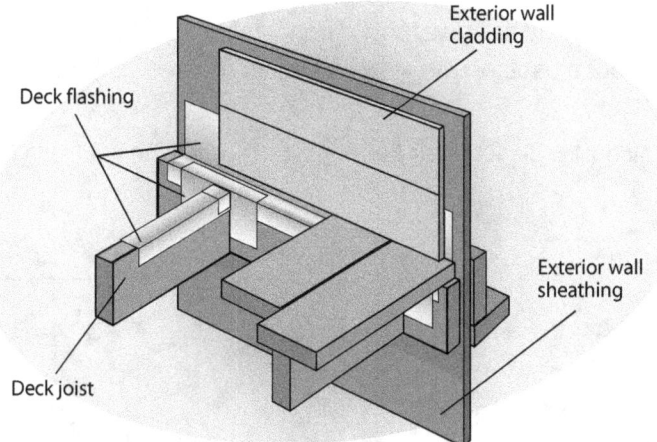

Figure 3. Deck flashing.

Guidance for Existing Decks and Other Attached Structures

To enhance the performance of existing decks and other attached structures, the following are recommended:

- Replace combustible materials with noncombustible or fire-resistant materials.

- Replace dimensional timber railings with railings constructed of fire-resistant materials such as metal, tempered glass, cables, or 3-inch nominal thickness fire-retardant-treated wood (see Figure 4).

- When the deck, balcony, stairs, or ramp can accommodate or be reinforced to accommodate additional load, install brick or concrete pavers and a suitable drainage mat over the existing decking (see Figure 4).

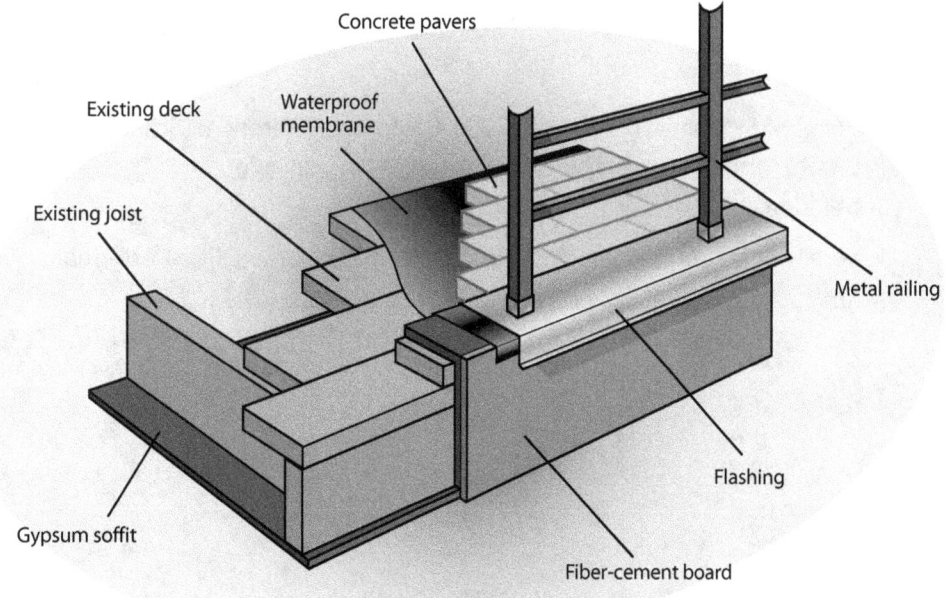

Figure 4. Concrete pavers over existing deck.

- Construct deck skirting around the deck using fire-resistant or noncombustible material such as fiber-cement boards and/or construct a patio on the ground around the deck, stairs, or ramp.
- Install a soffit at the underside of balconies, decks, stair landings, or ramps when skirting is not installed (see Figure 4).

Considerations

- Maintenance and removal of combustible debris and vegetation around and under decks and other attached structures is a key factor in reducing vulnerability to ignition during a wildfire (see Figure 5). For more information on defensible space, see Fact Sheet #4, Defensible Space.

- Decks and other attached structures should be maintained by replacing deteriorated components before they lose their fire-resistance.

- Decks enclosed with fire-resistant skirting must be vented for moisture control (see Fact Sheet #8, Vents).

Figure 5. Combustible debris under this deck ignited and led to the destruction of the deck. Although the siding is noncombustible, the fire spread from the deck through a window to the interior (firecenter. berkeley.edu).

Effectiveness

All mitigation measures listed in this Fact Sheet are effective in all Fire Severity Zones.

Resources

Decking: SFM Standard 12-7A-4. 2001 California Referenced Standard Codes (Part 12, Title 24, C.C.R.). http://www.fire.ca.gov/fire_prevention/downloads/Part_12_CA_SFM_12-7A-4_Test_Standards.pdf.

University of California Agriculture and Natural Resources. Fire Performance Testing: Decks. http://firecenter.berkeley.edu/quarles/deck_kit-SQ.pdf.

Landscape Fences and Walls

Purpose

To provide guidance about landscape fencing and walls that are attached to or near buildings in wildfire zones to reduce the potential for damage to the buildings from a wildfire.

Key Issues

- Landscape fences and walls function as physical or visual barriers or architectural statements. Property owners do not always consider the potential that landscape fences and walls can have in contributing to the spread of a wildfire.

- The common wooden post-and-board fence can become fuel for a wildfire, especially when the fence is old and weather-beaten. This type of fence can also collect embers and firebrands in a wildfire and act as a horizontal ladder fuel by allowing the fire to travel along the fence toward the main building (see Figure 1).

Figure 1. The gate that was attached to the garage at the corner ignited and led the fire to the home, causing the damage seen here (firecenter.berkeley. edu).

- Once ignited, a fence or wall constructed of combustible materials that is attached to or near a building can ignite the building through radiant or convective heat or by direct flame contact.

Guidance

- Use noncombustible materials for fences and walls. Fences and walls vary in shape, size, and construction materials, all of which provide varying degrees of protection or risk in a wildfire. Typical materials used in fences and walls are wood, plastic, composite, metal, wire, concrete, stone, and masonry. Of these materials, wood is the most combustible, while concrete, stone, and masonry are noncombustible.

  - *Wood.* Fences that are constructed of wood or have wooden components are combustible and therefore provide no fire resistance. Combustible materials such as soft woods and pine treated with preservatives should be avoided if the fence is attached to the building. Dense hardwoods such as red oak, white oak, hickory/pecan, and walnut are more fire-resistant than pines and other softwoods.

- *Plastic.* Plastic fences are more fire-resistant, more durable, and often stronger than wooden fences, but plastic fences can melt in a wildfire from temperatures that are below the maximum a wildfire can generate (see Figure 2).

- *Metal.* Metal fences are more fire-resistant than plastic fences. Wire fences such as barbed wire, hog wire, and chain link have little or no effect on fire passage. However, if combustible materials have accumulated in or around the fence or the fence contains combustible materials such as wooden posts, the fence can act as a horizontal ladder fuel by allowing the fire to travel along the fence toward the main building

Figure 2. Plastic fences can melt even under moderate wildfire temperatures (FEMA field team).

- *Concrete, stone, or masonry.* Concrete, stone, and masonry fences and walls are noncombustible and can act as a barrier to a wildfire by deflecting flames away from a building, but the passage of airborne embers and firebrands will not be significantly altered. These materials are the most effective at minimizing the potential for damage to a building from a wildfire.

• Avoid attaching fences and walls constructed of combustible materials to a building.

• For fences and walls that are attached to a building, ensure that all combustible components are at least 10 feet from the building to prevent heat and flames from igniting the building.

• Avoid fences that have gaps, such as wooden slat fences, because airborne firebrands can become trapped in the gaps and ignite the fence (see Figure 3).

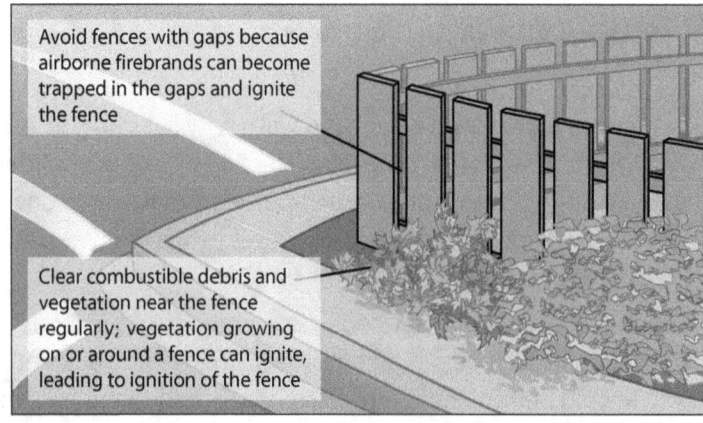

Avoid fences with gaps because airborne firebrands can become trapped in the gaps and ignite the fence

Clear combustible debris and vegetation near the fence regularly; vegetation growing on or around a fence can ignite, leading to ignition of the fence

Figure 3. Key guidance for fences.

Considerations

- The physical condition of the fence or wall should be maintained.
- Combustible debris near the fence or wall should be cleared regularly (see Fact Sheet #4, Defensible Space).
- The type of landscape vegetation that is planted next to a fence or wall should be considered, and the vegetation should be maintained regularly. Unmanaged landscape vegetation can increase the probability that the fence will ignite, especially a fence that is constructed of combustible materials (see Figure 3). For more information on defensible space, see Fact Sheet #4, Defensible Space.

Effectiveness

Masonry, concrete, stone, metal, and hardwood landscape fences and walls are effective in all Fire Severity Zones.

Resources

American Hardwood Information Center. http://www.hardwoodinfo.com/species_guide/brochure_44-45.pdf

Center for Fire Research and Outreach. University of California, Berkeley: College of Natural Resources. http://firecenter.berkeley.edu/default.htm.

Firesafe Council. http://www.firesafecouncil.org/.

Firewise Communities Program. http://www.firewise.org/.

Fire Sprinklers

Purpose

To provide guidance on the installation of interior and exterior fire sprinkler systems on buildings in wildfire zones. The guidance pertains to both new and existing buildings.

Key Issues

- During a wildfire, firebrands and airborne debris can breach windows, and convective heat and embers can penetrate utility openings, gaps around doors, and other openings. The interior of a building can ignite even when the exterior does not. Fire sprinklers are not common in residential construction, but they can be effective in preventing damage from a wildfire.

- Exterior building components that are combustible such as overhangs and recessed alcoves can trap embers, firebrands, and hot gases, leading to ignition of the building. Exterior sprinklers can help extinguish flames before the building has been substantially damaged.

- A building that has ignited can endanger nearby buildings and contribute to the spread of a wildfire. Interior and exterior sprinklers can prevent substantial damage to the building, protect nearby buildings, and prevent the fire from igniting nearby combustible vegetation.

Interior Fire Sprinklers

Common Misconception	Fact
All sprinklers in a system activate simultaneously.	Only sprinkler heads that are in an area of high heat are activated. Typically, only one or two heads activate during a fire. Sprinkler heads are activated only by heat, not by smoke.
Sprinklers can activate accidentally.	According to the U.S. Fire Administration, only 1 in 16 million sprinkler heads activates accidentally.
Water damage from sprinklers is more expensive to repair than damage from the fire.	Water damage from sprinklers is usually considerably less expensive to repair than damage caused by water from fire hoses, smoke, and fire. Quick-response sprinklers release 8 to 24 gallons of water per minute, while fire hoses release 50 to 125 gallons per minute.
Interior sprinkler systems are obtrusive and not aesthetically pleasing in residences.	Interior fire sprinklers for single-family residences are smaller than traditional commercial or industrial fire sprinklers and can be coordinated with any room décor. Sprinkler heads come in a variety of styles, models, and colors and can be mounted flush with the ceiling (see Figure 1) or concealed behind covers.

Characteristics

- Interior fire sprinkler systems can detect a developing fire quickly and activate automatically. Systems do not require manual intervention.
- Interior sprinkler systems can include a warning system that notifies occupants and emergency response personnel of a developing fire.
- Interior sprinklers can be installed during new construction or in an existing home.

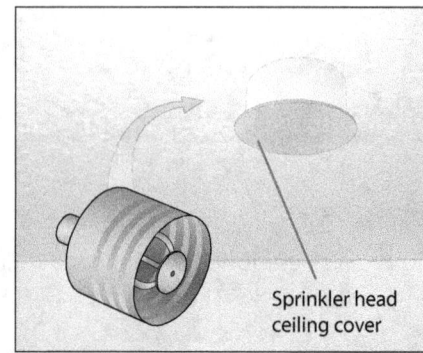

Figure 1. A concealed, aesthetically pleasing fire sprinkler.

Guidance

- Installing sprinklers in unoccupied, enclosed spaces such as attics should be considered because doing so can provide additional protection if fire penetrates the exterior of the space.
- Water pressure and supply must both be adequate for an interior sprinkler system to be effective. Water is typically supplied by the water main from the municipal water supply. During a wildfire, firefighting resources often exhaust the available water pressure. If existing water pressure is inadequate or the source of water is a well, a holding tank can be used as a water source. To ensure that water is available to the system during a wildfire, a pressurized holding tank should be considered, even if the structure is connected to the municipal water supply.

Considerations

- The majority of the cost of an interior sprinkler system is associated with the piping material. Options for materials include steel alloys, copper, and fire-resistant plastics. Plastic piping is less expensive than steel alloys and copper, but its melting point is as much as five times lower than copper piping.
- Hazard insurance rates are typically discounted for homes with interior sprinkler systems.
- An interior sprinkler system is relatively easy to install during new construction. The system increases the total cost of construction by approximately 2 percent; complex and multi-story installations may increase the cost more. Installing an interior sprinkler system can be done when the roof is replaced or upgraded, and doing so may cost less than standard installation.
- The cost of installing an interior sprinkler system during new construction is about half the cost of installing a system in an existing building.

Effectiveness

Internal sprinklers extinguish the fire at an early stage and prevent substantial damage from heat and smoke or total loss of the structure. They are effective in all Fire Severity Zones.

Exterior Fire Sprinklers

Characteristics

- The purpose of an exterior fire sprinkler system is to saturate the exterior of the building.
- Exterior sprinkler systems can be installed during new construction or on existing buildings. They are commonly installed on the roof along the ridge line or underneath the eaves and along soffits.
- Exterior sprinklers can be activated automatically by low-voltage heat detectors or manually by occupants before they evacuate the home.
- Exterior sprinklers can include a warning system that notifies occupants and emergency response personnel of a developing fire.
- Some landscape sprinklers are designed and installed to provide protection from a wildfire to landscape areas immediately surrounding a building.
- An exterior sprinkler system can be installed so that it is substantially hidden from view.

Guidance

Exterior sprinklers mounted on the building can be configured to use water piping through the attic or roof or to use piping on the exterior of the structure. If interior pipes are used, exterior sprinklers can be installed in conjunction with interior sprinklers (see Figure 2). A stand-alone system that includes a pressurized holding tank can be considered to ensure an adequate water supply. See the information about water supply under interior fire sprinklers above.

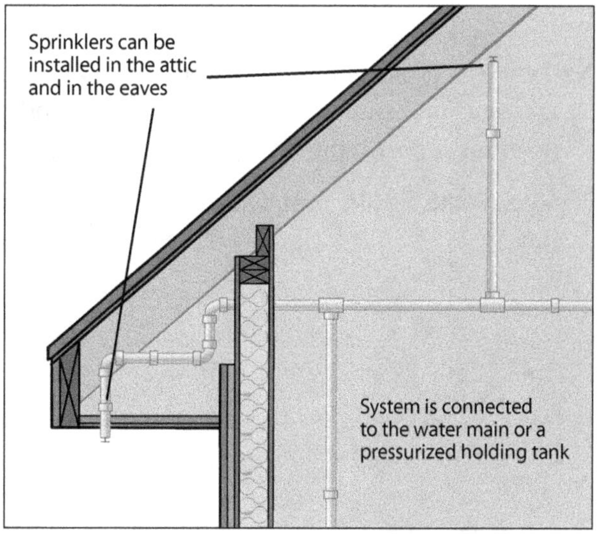

Sprinklers can be installed in the attic and in the eaves

System is connected to the water main or a pressurized holding tank

Figure 2. Interior and exterior fire sprinklers can be installed in conjunction with each other, such as this system with a sprinkler in the attic and along the eave.

Considerations

- If exterior sprinklers are installed in areas where freezing temperatures occur, special provisions such as dry sprinklers are required to prevent water in the piping from freezing and rupturing it. In a dry sprinkler system, the portion of piping that is vulnerable to freezing is not charged with water until a fire opens a valve and releases water into the piping.
- Exterior sprinklers can provide added protection when used in conjunction with fire-resistant construction materials (see Fact Sheets #5–14) and defensible space (see Fact Sheet #4, Defensible Space).
- Polymer gels, Class A foam products, and other long-term fire retardants can be applied to structures prior to fire impingement and provide greater thermal protection than water alone.

Many of these products are available to homeowners in self-contained application units and can be applied with an attachment to a garden hose or integrated into the home's exterior sprinkler systems.

Effectiveness

- If exterior fire sprinklers require manual activation, occupants must activate the system expeditiously for the system to be effective.
- High winds that are frequently a byproduct of major fire activity can significantly degrade the effectiveness of an exterior sprinkler system.
- Manually applied fire-protection materials such as Class A foam products can be effective if time is available to treat the home. To be effective, the fire-protection material must be applied within the time frame identified by the product manufacturer.

Resources

FireSafety.gov. *Residential Fire Sprinklers*. http://www.firesafety.gov/citizens/ sprinklers/index. shtm.

National Fire Protection Association. 2007. NFPA 13D: *Standard for the Installation of Sprinkler Systems in One- and Two-Family Dwellings and Manufactured Homes*. http://www.nfpa.org/ aboutthecodes/AboutTheCodes.asp?DocNum=13D.

National Fire Sprinkler Association. Information about residential sprinkler systems. http://www. nfsa.org.

Utilities and Exterior Equipment

Purpose

To provide information about measures that can be implemented to protect utility connections to buildings and exterior equipment from a wildfire. Guidance pertains to both new and existing buildings.

Description

Utilities of all types that penetrate a building can be a threat to a building in a wildfire. Exterior equipment, such as solar panels and receiver dishes, can be vulnerable to damage by the high temperatures generated by a wildfire. The following utilities and equipment are particularly susceptible to damage in a wildfire:

Electrical Utilities and Exterior Equipment

Electricity is delivered to homes through aboveground conductors and drop lines (the majority of homes) or through underground cables. Electricity is then provided to exterior equipment by cables that are connected to the equipment from inside the home.

Fuel-related Utilities and Exterior Equipment

Many homes use pressurized gas (liquid petroleum gas, such as propane and butane, or natural gas) or liquid fuel (fuel oil or kerosene) for heating, hot water, and cooking. Propane and butane are stored in pressurized vessels. Natural gas is delivered through pressurized pipes that are connected to the home. Liquid fuel is delivered to the home by gravity from on-site storage tanks.

Key Issues

General

- Exterior equipment often contains combustible components that increase the risk of ignition of the equipment and the building it is attached to.
- Most utilities and exterior equipment require penetration of the building envelope for ducting and conduit (see Figure 1). The openings may allow heat, hot gases, and embers to enter the building and cause ignition of combustible materials in the building interior.

Figure 1. The gap around utility penetrations such as this one should be filled.

- Combustible debris can collect around exterior equipment, increasing the probability of ignition of the equipment and building.

Electrical Utilities and Equipment

- Wildfires can affect power transmission by conduction, convection, direct flame contact, and heavy smoke. Wildfires can damage equipment such as power poles and power lines or cause a short circuit in the lines.
- Power surges and power outages caused by wind and fire can damage electrically powered equipment in homes that are miles away.
- As with any electrical power supply, water well power supplies are vulnerable during a wildfire. Water well systems can be essential to domestic and fire-protection needs.
- Equipment mounted on roofs has the same ignition potential as the roofing assembly.

Fuel-related Utilities and Equipment

- Exposed, combustible delivery lines are vulnerable to wildfire. For example, gas meters are vulnerable to wildfire damage if pipe connections include a rubberized gasket.
- Pressurized and liquid fuels are flammable and explosive.
- Venting of fuel under pressure may cause significant damage or total destruction of a building, depending primarily on the location of the fuel container.

Guidance

General

- If possible, install utility and equipment connections underground, including all entry points into the building.
- If a utility or equipment connection cannot be installed underground, seal gaps and penetrations in exterior walls and roofs with fire-resistant caulk, mortar, or fire-rated expanding foam. Fill large gaps with intumescent or fire-protective sheets or pillows. Fire-resistant wrap may be used around ventilation features that are built into and penetrate exterior walls (such as air conditioners).

Electrical Utilities and Equipment

- Shield power cables and other wiring with noncombustible or fire-resistant materials to protect the cables and wiring from convection, radiation, and conduction heat, and direct flame contact.
- Use noncombustible or fire-resistant materials for mounting systems of roof-mounted equipment.
- Use surge protectors to protect sensitive electronic equipment.

- Install Class A rated solar cell systems for the greatest protection. Solar cell systems are tested and rated under the same conditions as roofing assemblies and are available with Class A and Class C ratings (see Fact Sheet #5, Roofs).

Fuel-related Utilities and Equipment

- Bury or shield fuel lines to protect them from radiation, conduction heat, and direct flame contact.

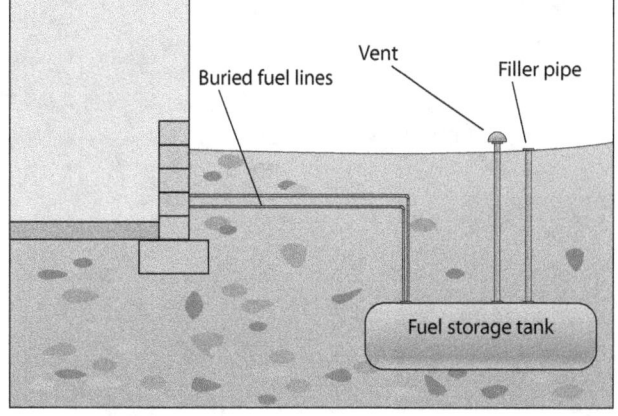

Figure 2. Buried fuel storage tank.

- Bury pressurized storage vessels underground (see Figure 2).
- Place fuel storage vessels 30 feet from the home and away from downhill slopes and enclose them behind a noncombustible masonry wall.
- Shield gas meters from hot air and gases, convection and radiant heat, and direct contact by flame, using noncombustible materials such as masonry or concrete.
- Ensure pressurized storage tanks have a pressure relief valve. As the outside temperature rises in a wildfire, the pressure inside the tank can increase. When the pressure setting is exceeded, the valve will open and relieve the pressure, preventing an explosion.

Considerations

- Replacing pipes, cables, and other installations can damage sealants for wall penetrations. Fire-resistant sealants and noncombustible mortar must be removed and replaced each time a cable or pipe is reinstalled.
- Using defensible space for the location of utilities and exterior equipment (for example, electric water pumps, fuel tanks) should be considered (see Fact Sheet #4, Defensible Space).

Effectiveness

All measures listed in this Fact Sheet are effective in all Fire Severity Zones.

Resources

Fire-resistant expanding foam standards: ASTM E814, UL 1479, BS 476, Part 20.

Pressure relief valve standards: ASME (American Society of Mechanical Engineers) Boiler & Pressure Vessel Code, Section VIII Division 1 and Section I.

Community Infrastructure

Purpose

To provide guidance about neighborhood and community-wide fire-safe practices that will enhance fire protection in wildfire zones. Guidance pertains to community infrastructure, including roads used for evacuation routes and emergency access, and emergency water supply. Although a home builder may not have control over these elements, community officials and homeowners should be aware of measures that can be taken on a community-wide basis to increase the chances of an entire neighborhood's survival in a wildfire.

Background

- Poorly designed or inadequate infrastructure can hamper fire-suppression efforts and put citizens and firefighters at risk. Reducing the risk of wildfire damage and destruction requires implementing measures beyond those involving an individual building or parcel. It is also essential to enhance mitigation measures at the neighborhood and community levels, which will effectively expand the zone of protection beyond the individual parcel or building.

- The local fire agency, state forestry or natural resources departments, the local office of emergency management, or other local organizations should be contacted to obtain information about the hazards and risks in an area.

Key Issues

- Emergency response vehicles may need to access a wildfire area at the same time evacuation traffic is leaving the area. Firefighters need safe access along roads to reach the wildfire and access water resources.

- Visible street signs and property addresses provide firefighters with critical response and location information. Property addresses are often not visible, and a road name may occur more than once in a jurisdiction.

- Wildland fuels and landscape vegetation along roads can place firefighters in extremely hazardous situations.

- Water resources for wildfire suppression are vital and need to be accessible.

Guidance for Roads and Driveways

- Roads should be wide enough to allow evacuation and emergency vehicles simultaneous access. Minimum width is 20 feet for access roads and 12 feet for driveways (see Figure 1).

- The maximum grade of roads and driveways should be determined by the local jurisdiction but in general should not exceed a grade of 16 percent.

- Roads and driveways should provide sufficient vertical clearance to allow for large emergency vehicles. The minimum is 13.6 feet (see Figure 1).

- Roads should support a minimum of 40,000 pounds to allow for heavy emergency vehicles.

- Appropriate signage, including but not limited to weight and vertical clearance limitations and one-way road and single-lane conditions, should be posted and fully visible on noncombustible signs and posts.

- Gated access from a public roadway should be set back from the roadway at a distance that is sufficient to allow emergency equipment to clear the traffic lane. A distance of 50 feet should be adequate for most equipment (see Figure 2).

- Turnarounds should be at the end of roads and on driveways that are longer than 150 feet. The minimum inside turning radius should not be less than 30 feet, and the outside turning radius for a turnaround should be 45 feet from the center line of the road. If a hammerhead/"T" is used, the top of the "T" should have a minimum length of 60 feet (see Figure 3).

- Roads and driveways should provide all-weather access, which may require asphalt or concrete surfacing.

Figure 1. Road with adequate width for emergency vehicles.

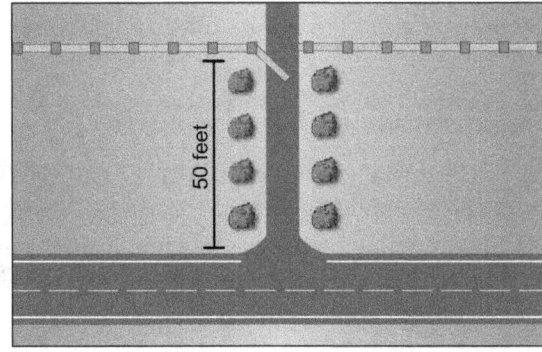

Figure 2. Gated access with a 50-foot setback that allows emergency vehicles to clear the traffic lane.

Figure 3. The top of the "T" used for a turnaround (Anchor Point Group, Boulder, CO).

Address and Signage

- Public and private roads and streets should be identified by a name or number through a consistent jurisdiction-wide system that provides for sequenced or patterned numbering and/or non-duplicating naming within each jurisdiction.

- Size of letters, numbers, and symbols for street and road signs should have a minimum 4-inch letter height and 1/2-inch stroke, be reflective, and contrast with the background color of the sign. The sign and sign support should be constructed of noncombustible materials.

- Street and road signs should be visible and legible from both directions of vehicle travel for a distance of at least 100 feet and be mounted at a height of 7 feet from the road surface to the bottom of the sign.

- All buildings should have a permanently posted address at each driveway entrance and should be visible from both directions of travel along the access road.

Fuel Modification

- Reducing the volume and density of combustible vegetation reduces the intensity of wildfire. Strategic fuel modification along access and egress routes increases safety for emergency fire equipment and evacuating citizens (see Figure 4).

- Areas such as golf courses, schools, and large parking lots should be labeled as safety zones for citizens unable to evacuate or for firefighters. It is critically important that these areas be evaluated by fire professionals before a safety zone is designated.

Figure 4. Example of a map depicting areas for planned fuel modification along evacuation routes/fire access roads (Anchor Point Group, Boulder, CO).

Guidance for Emergency Water Supply

- Community-wide water supplies need to be available and accessible.

- Signs should be provided indicating access to each water source.

- Vegetation should be maintained at each water source to allow safe access to the source.

Water Tanks and Pressure Systems

Some community water systems use tanks and cisterns to store emergency water supplies. Individual properties may be supplied with potable water through on-site wells or limited distribution systems due to the dispersed nature of the community or the cost of installing a major water delivery system.

- Water tanks should be constructed of highly fire-resistant materials such as steel, concrete, or ferrocement. Fiberglass tanks may be placed underground. All cisterns or water tanks used for emergencies should have a fire department connection. The local jurisdiction may specify the size and type of fire department connection.

- Pressurized systems with hydrants should conform to the local jurisdiction's requirements or recommendations for spacing, flow, and pressure.

- Installation should meet National Fire Protection Association standards at the minimum.

Dry Hydrants

Many rural areas do not have access to the pressurized hydrants that are common in larger communities for firefighting. When pressurized systems are not available, dry hydrants are recommended. Dry hydrants are a relatively inexpensive way to provide a ready source of water for firefighting

A dry hydrant is a non-pressurized pipe system that allows fire equipment access to a nearby source of water such as a lake, stream, pond, residential pool, or cistern with a minimum water depth of 2 feet, or a water source such as a tank that is not directly accessible to a fire apparatus (see Figure 5).

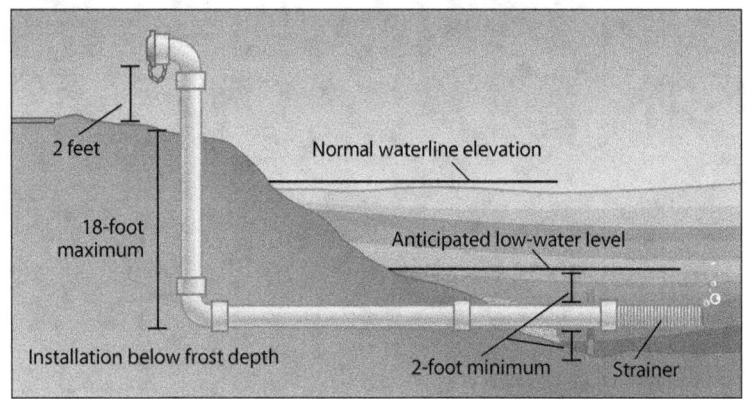
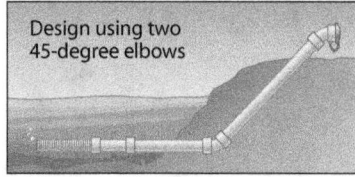
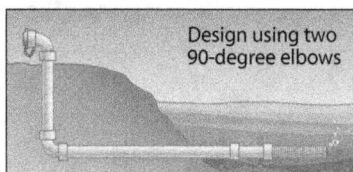

Figure 5. Dry hydrant designs.

Considerations

The fire-suppression capabilities in the area, as discussed above, should be considered when selecting a construction site (see Fact Sheet #3, Selecting the Construction Site).

For more information about infrastructure, see FEMA's *Wildfire Hazard Mitigation Handbook for Public Facilities*.

Effectiveness

The effectiveness of the recommended measures varies significantly, depending on the infrastructure elements that are present in the community.

Resources

California Administrative Code Title 14, Division 1.5, §1270–1276.

International Code Council. 2006. *2006 International Wildland-Urban Interface Code.*

National Fire Protection Association. 2001. *NFPA Standard 1142: Standard on Water Supplies for Suburban and Rural Fire Fighting.*

Natural Resources Conservation Service. Dry Hydrant Design Drawings. http://www.sc.nrcs.usda.gov/technical/dryhydrant.html.

Lagucki, T. and K. Mancl. Fire Protection in Rural Areas: Dry Hydrants for Ponds. The Ohio State University Fact Sheet: Food, Agricultural and Biological Engineering. http://ohioline.osu.edu/aex-fact/0422.html.

Rancho Santa Fe [California] Fire Protection District. Standard for Driveways, Dead-Ends and Looped Access Ways. http://www.rsf-fire.org/prevention/access_requirements.asp. Includes information on fire access road and fire hydrant specifications (specifications and ordinances may be different for other states, cities, and districts).

State of Minnesota. The Dry Hydrant Concept. http://files.dnr.state.mn.us/ assistance/backyard/firewise/dryhydrant_advantages.pdf.

Winter, A., S. Holman, S. Kett, and R. Dolan. 2006. *Taylor [Florida] Community Wildfire Protection Plan.* http://www.fl-dof.com/publications/fire_pdfs/taylor_fl_cwpp_complete.pdf. Includes improvements to wildland fire response, such as installation of dry hydrants and upgrades to communications equipment.